L-16866

8-17115

C000020492

Making
Country
Classic
Tinware

Making Country Classic Tinware

Catherine
Austin

A Sterling/Chapelle Book
Sterling Publishing Co., Inc. New York

The photographs in this book were taken at
Trends & Traditions, Ogden, Utah;
Treasure Basket, Ogden, Utah;
Bloomingsales, Salt Lake City, Utah;
and at the homes of Jo Packham and Edie Stockstill.
Their cooperation and trust are greatly appreciated.

Library of Congress Catologing-in-Publication Data

Austin, Catherine.
    Making country classic tinware / by Catherine Austin.
        p.   cm.
    "A Sterling/Chapelle book."
    Includes index.
    ISBN 0-8069-0398-8
    1. Tinsmithing. 2. Handicraft. I. Title.
TT266.A97   1993
739.5'32—dc20   93-12798
                                    CIP

10 9 8 7 6 5 4 3 2 1

A Sterling/Chapelle Book

Published by Sterling Publishing Company, Inc.
387 Park Avenue South, New York, N.Y. 10016
© 1993 by Chapelle Ltd.
Distributed in Canada by Sterling Publishing
c/o Canadian Manda Group, P.O. Box 920, Station U
Toronto, Ontario, Canada M8Z 5P9
Distributed in Great Britain and Europe by Cassell PLC
Villiers House, 41/47 Strand, London WC2N 5JE, England
Distributed in Australia by Capricorn Link Ltd.
P.O. Box 665, Lane Cove, NSW 2066
Printed and bound in Hong Kong
All rights reserved

Sterling ISBN 0-8069-0398-8

__Owner__
Jo Packham

__Staff__
Trice Boerens
Tina Annette Brady
Sheri Lynn Castle
Holly Fuller
Kristi Glissmeyer
Cherie Hanson
Susan Jorgensen
Margaret Shields Marti
Jackie McCowen
Barbara Milburn
Kathleen R. Montoya
Pamela Randall
Jennifer Roberts
Florence Stacey
Lew Stoddard
Nancy Whitley
Gloria Zirkel

__Designers__
Amber Fuller
Jo Packham
Jennifer Roberts
David Stacey
Florence Stacey
Scott Stacey
Edie Stockstill

__Photography__
Ryne Hazen

Contents

✦ ❖ ✦

*Passed down for many generations as a
useful science, tinware gradually drifted into
the realm of folk art. Now it is enjoying a
resurgence in popularity. And it is no wonder!
Working with tinware only looks difficult. With
a few simple tools, the necessary techniques are
quickly mastered, as you will discover after
creating a few of the designs in this book.*

*First, familiarize yourself with the General
Instructions beginning on page 139. This section
explains everything you will need to know about
tools, materials and techniques. In modern usage,
"tinware" includes aluminum, brass and copper.
Once you get to know these soft, pliable metals,
you will handle them easily.*

*This book requires no special skills, it is meant
for beginners and accomplished craftspersons alike.
Quick and enjoyable to make, these projects will
inspire you to create your own unique designs,
adding the warmth and charm of old folk art
to your home.*

✦ ❖ ✦

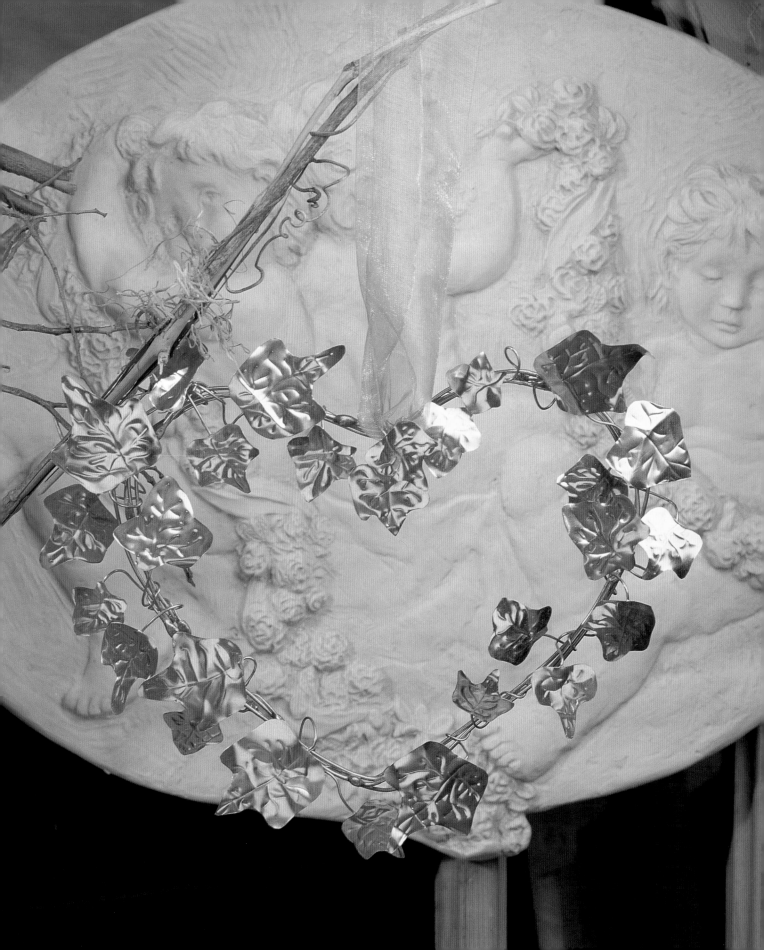

Entwined Heart

MATERIALS

6 feet of 14-gauge
    copper wire
5 feet of 18-gauge
    copper wire
3 feet of 20-gauge
    copper wire
12" square of 36-gauge
    tooling copper
Copper paint
Matte spray
Needle-nose pliers
Soldering iron and solder

DIRECTIONS

1. Cut 14-gauge wire into three 24" lengths. Bend each length into a heart shape. Solder ends of each heart together.

2. Layer the three hearts together. Wrap the 20-gauge wire tightly around the hearts to secure. Cut excess wire and solder the ends of the 20-gauge wire together.

3. Transfer fourteen large and fourteen small leaf patterns onto copper. With right side up, place copper on a stack of paper. Emboss veins according to patterns. Cut out leaves.

4. Cut 18-gauge wire into twenty-eight 2" lengths. Solder one wire to the back center of each leaf.

5. Using needle-nose pliers, wrap wire tails at 1" intervals around wreath frame. Vary the length of each tail; see photo. Solder wire tails in place to wreath frame. Cover soldering spots with copper paint. Allow to dry. Finish with matte spray.

SMALL LEAF

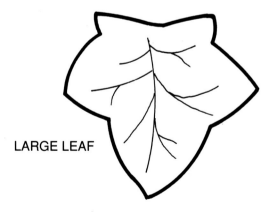

LARGE LEAF

Sweetheart Sachet

MATERIALS

⅜ yard of print fabric
7" square of 36-gauge
   tooling copper
3 feet of 24-gauge wire
18" of 18-gauge copper wire
Heavyweight copper-colored
   rayon thread
Potpourri
Polyester stuffing
Hammer
⅛" awl

DIRECTIONS

1. Make fabric heart pattern by adding 2" all around to the heart on page 12. Cut two large hearts from fabric. With right sides facing, stitch using a ¼" seam; leave a 2" opening. Clip seam allowance at cleavage; turn. Stuff moderately with potpourri and polyester stuffing. Slipstitch opening closed.

2. Transfer heart pattern on page 12 onto copper. With right side up, place on a stack of paper. Emboss according to pattern. Punch holes with awl where indicated. Cut out.

3. Stitch copper heart to heart pillow securely, pulling rayon thread through holes in copper heart. Set aside.

4. Bend 18-gauge copper wire into a star according to pattern. Wrap star with 24-gauge copper wire.

5. To make hanger, double thread and stitch an 8" length at top center of curve on each side of heart. Tie ends of thread around the star; see photo.

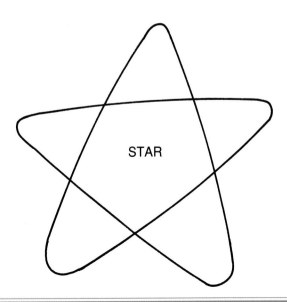

STAR

*page
12*

HEART

My Sweet Valentine

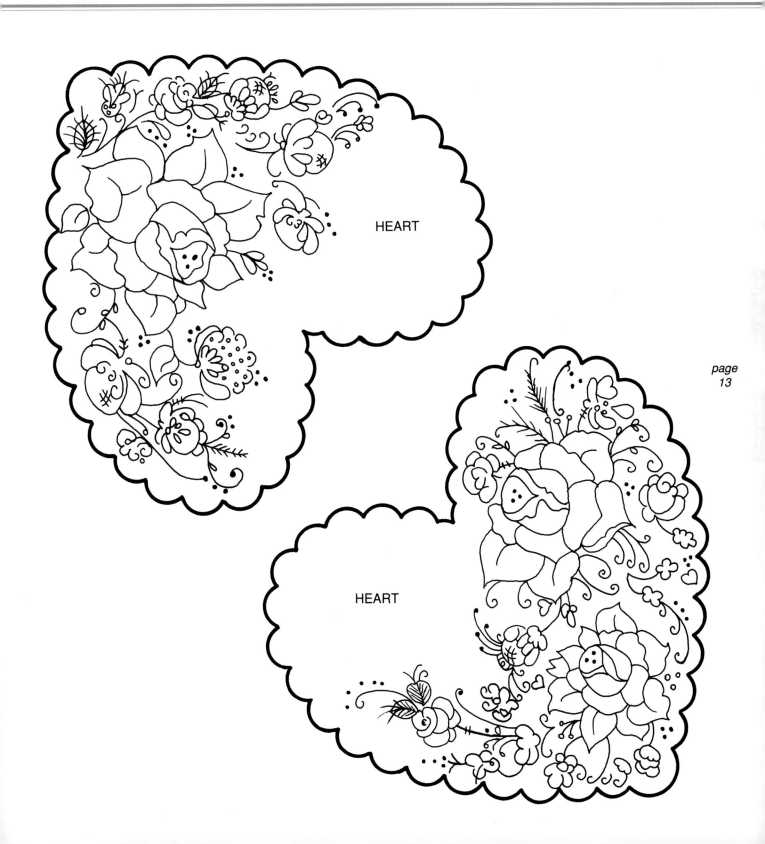

HEART

page
13

HEART

MATERIALS

12" x 17" sheet of 36-gauge
  tooling copper
26" of 10-gauge copper wire
Acrylic paints: green, mauve,
  pink, red, white
200 red seed beads
Matte spray
Super glue
Soldering iron and solder

DIRECTIONS

1. Transfer heart pattern outline six times onto copper. With right side up, place copper on a stack of paper. Emboss each heart with one pattern, using each pattern twice. Find more patterns on page 13. Cut out.

2. Shape wire into an 8"-diameter circle. Place hearts, cleavage-side out, around wire circle as desired. Solder the back of each heart to the wire circle; see photo.

3. Paint roses and leaves as desired; see photo. Allow to dry. Finish with matte spray.

4. Glue seed beads on as desired. Finish with matte spray.

HEART

Prrrfect Angel

MATERIALS

12" x 36" sheet of 36-gauge
   tooling copper
Assorted acrylic paints
Matte spray
Super glue

DIRECTIONS

1. Transfer one cat and two wing patterns on pages 18 and 19 onto copper. Cut out.

2. Paint according to pattern with desired colors. Allow to dry. Finish with matte spray.

3. Center and glue wings behind wings on cat pattern.

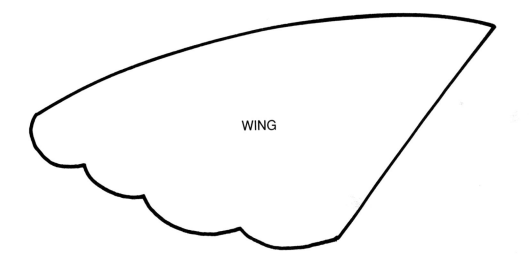

WING

ANGEL CAT

Easter Egg Caddies

MATERIALS

3" x 5" sheet of 36-gauge
    tooling copper
2" x 5½" sheet of 36-gauge
    tooling brass
Soldering iron and solder

DIRECTIONS

1. Transfer one duck and one rabbit pattern onto copper. Cut out. Set aside. Cut two 1" x 5½" strips from brass.

2. To make bands, bend each brass strip into a circle. Overlap ends ½" and attach a paper clip to hold together. Place seam side down, and solder ends together, avoiding the paper clip. Remove the paper clip. Solder one animal cutout to the seam on each band.

DUCK

RABBIT

Home Forever

MATERIALS

8" x 10" sheet of 36-gauge
  tooling brass
Three to five brass or
  copper jewelry pieces
6" of 20-gauge copper wire
Primer spray
Metallic gold paint
Matte spray
Super glue
Hammer
⅛" awl
Heavy-duty craft knife

DIRECTIONS

1. Transfer house pattern on page 24 onto brass. With wrong side up, place copper on a stack of paper. Emboss scoring lines and punch two small holes according to pattern. Using a craft knife, cut out doorway on house. Cut out house.

2. Fold house in on scored lines. Glue roof and base along seams.

3. Coat house with primer spray. Allow to dry. Paint the entire house with metallic gold paint. Allow to dry.

4. Shape copper wire into a star according to pattern. Insert open end of star into holes on roof. Glue in place and touch up with paint. Glue jewelry pieces onto house as desired. Finish with matte spray.

STAR

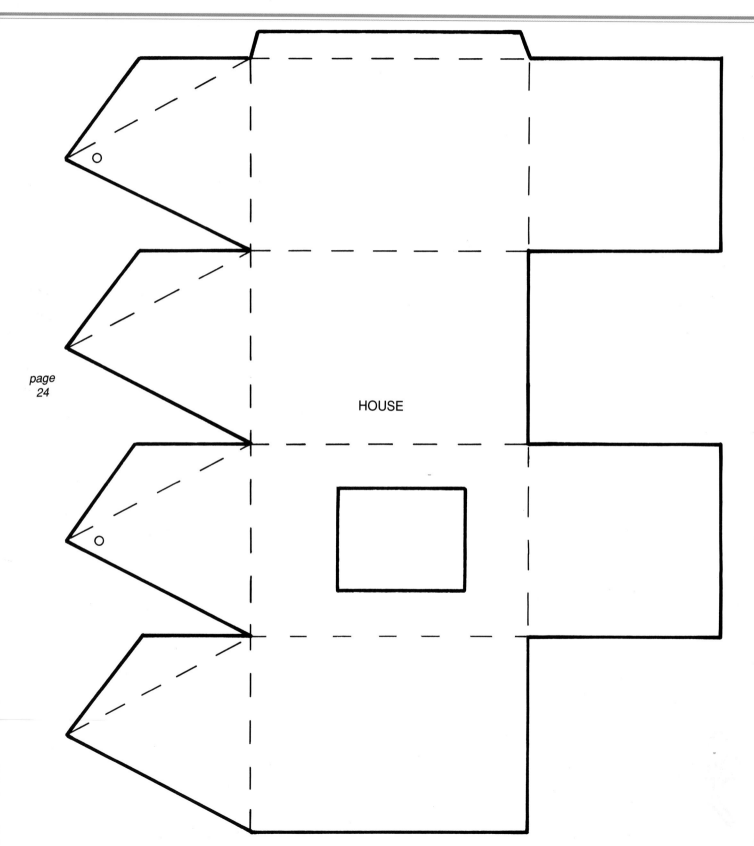

page
24

HOUSE

Ivy Leaf Loft

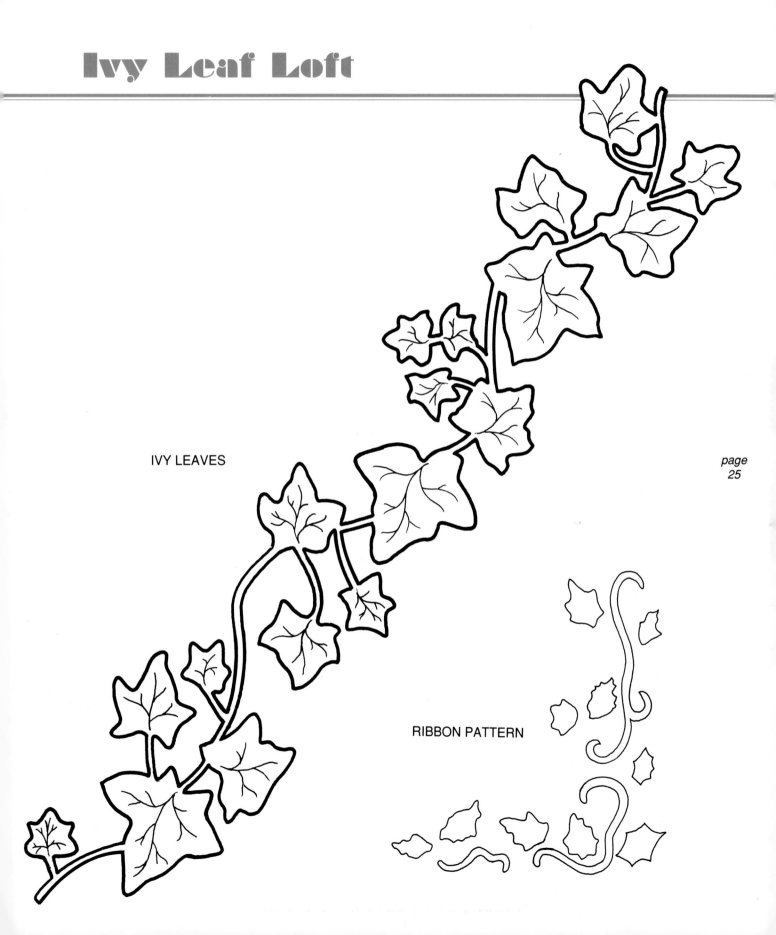

IVY LEAVES

page 25

RIBBON PATTERN

MATERIALS

Two 4" x 4½" x ¾"
    purchased wooden hearts
12" x 36" sheet of 36-gauge
    tooling copper
54" of 24-gauge copper wire
6" of 14-gauge copper wire
Copper tacks
Two ½"-long nails
Green acrylic paint
Liver of sulphur
Needle-nose pliers
Soldering iron and solder
Electric drill with ⅛" and ¾"
    drill bits
Tin snips

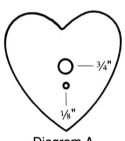

Diagram A

Diagram B

DIRECTIONS

1. Drill a ⅛" and a ¾" hole in one wooden heart, according to Diagram A.

2. From copper, cut one 5" x 15" strip. Using wooden heart as a pattern, cut out two copper hearts, each 1" larger than the original. With wrong side up, place copper hearts on a stack of paper. Emboss with ribbon pattern on page 25. Using a craft knife, cut out a ½" hole in one copper heart. Cut ¼" snips around hole, according to Diagram B.

3. Cut short snips around the edges of copper hearts at ¼" intervals, according to Diagram B. Bend snipped edges up. Place copper heart with hole over wooden heart with hole. Bend snipped edges of hole in copper heart into hole in wooden heart. Tap the edges of the copper heart with a hammer to hold in place. Repeat with remaining copper and wooden heart.

4. With one heart at either end, shape the 5" x 15" strip to fit around the hearts. Ends should meet at the bottom tip of hearts. Using a hammer and copper tacks, tack the copper strip into place along the edge of the hearts. Fold one end over the other; tack in place. Hammer one nail at cleavage of heart, leaving nail head raised. Repeat with other nail at opposite cleavage.

5. For handle, cut the 24-gauge copper into three 18" lengths. Using needle-nose pliers, twist the three lengths together. Wrap either end of the twisted wire around raised nails at heart cleavage.

6. For perch, fold 14-gauge wire in half and twist. Insert raw ends into ⅛" hole.

7. Transfer ivy pattern on page 25 four times onto copper. With wrong side up, place copper on a stack of paper. Emboss veins according to pattern. Cut out.

8. Apply liver of sulphur to bird house and ivy. Allow to dry. Highlight with steel wool.

9. Paint right side of ivy green. Allow to dry. Highlight with steel wool to bring out veins. Gently wrap ivy around twisted handle.

Sweetwater Farm

MATERIALS

24" square of 24-gauge
    tooling copper
6" square of 36-gauge tooling
    brass
5½" of 24-gauge copper wire
Super glue
Hammer
⅛" awl
Soldering iron and solder
Tin snips

DIRECTIONS

1. Enlarge and transfer two house patterns on page 30 onto copper. Also transfer two roof patterns on page 31 onto copper. Cut out. Set aside. Transfer medium bird and small oval patterns onto copper. Cut out. Set aside.

2. Transfer one large, two medium and one small bird pattern onto brass. Transfer door and window patterns on page 30 onto brass. Cut out all shapes. Set aside.

3. Place house sections on a flat surface facing opposite directions. Emboss scoring lines on each section according to pattern. Fold sections toward scoring lines. When houses are placed long sides together, seams should be facing the same side. Cut

out door on front of one house and window on front of other house, according to pattern. See diagram.

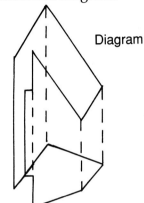

Diagram

4. Place roof sections on a flat surface facing opposite directions. Emboss scoring lines on each section. Fold sections in toward scoring lines.

5. To assemble each house section, solder long tab to the inside of long edge. Place house sections long sides together with seams in the back.

6. Place one roof section on corresponding house section so that 1" extends along front side. Glue roof to tabs on top of house. Glue roof tabs to back edge and long side edge of house. Repeat with remaining roof section and corresponding house section.

7. Glue brass birds and ornaments to front of house; see photo.

8. To make weather vane, glue copper bird to one end of 5½" wire. Using an awl, punch a small hole in the center of the copper oval piece. Slide oval piece over the wire, 1" from free end. Glue in place. Solder the wire to one long side of the house below oval.

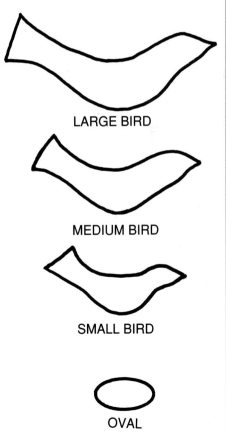

LARGE BIRD

MEDIUM BIRD

SMALL BIRD

OVAL

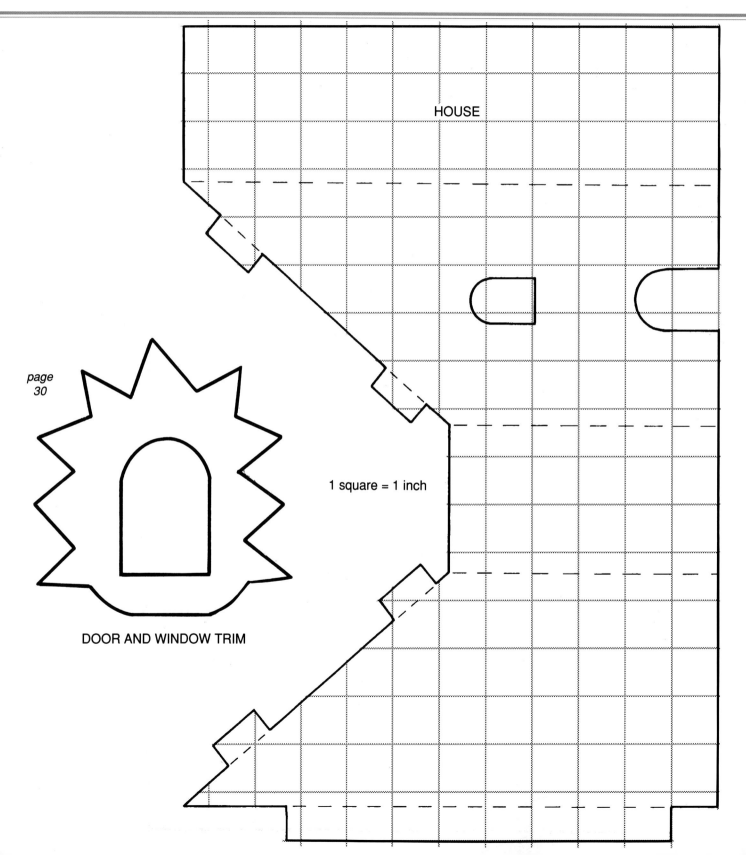

HOUSE

page
30

1 square = 1 inch

DOOR AND WINDOW TRIM

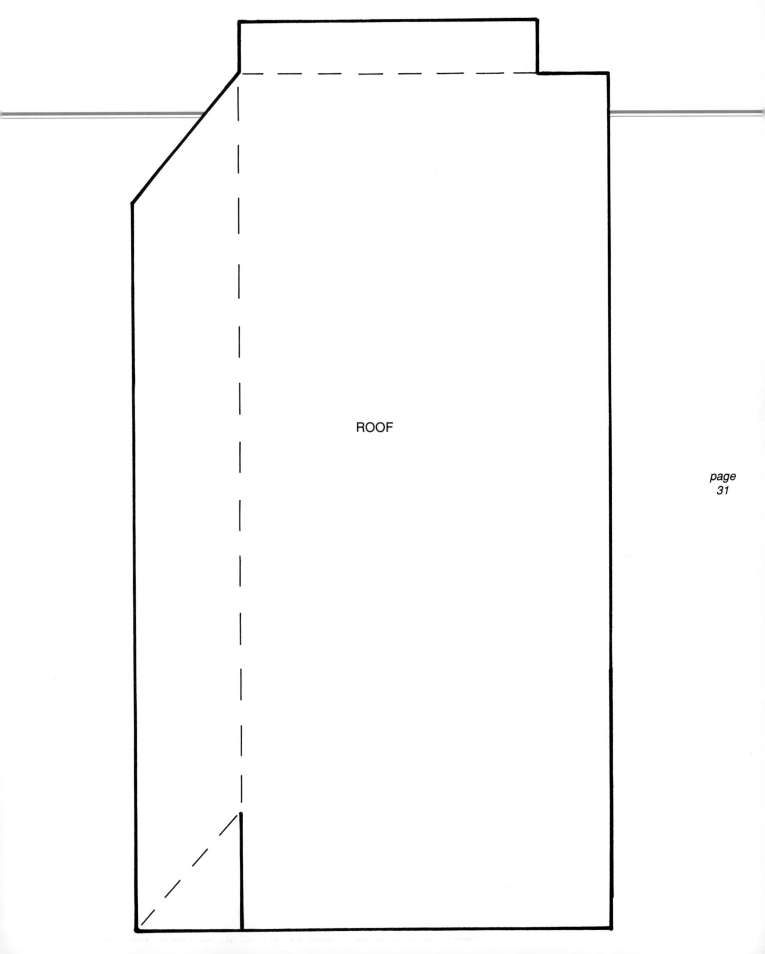

ROOF

Return from Pasture

MATERIALS

12" square of 36-gauge
  tooling copper
22" of 12-gauge copper wire
25" of 18-gauge copper wire
Copper patina
Matte spray
Needle-nose pliers
Soldering iron and solder

DIRECTIONS

1. Transfer cow pattern five times onto copper. Cut out.

2. Cut 18-gauge wire into five 5" lengths. Making sure that all cows are facing the same direction, solder one length of wire to the bottom center back of each cow. Leave 4" wire tails extending.

3. Lay the 12-gauge wire out straight. Using needle-nose pliers, wrap 3" of the wire tail of one cow 2" from the edge of the 12-gauge wire. Wrap the remaining cows in the same manner at 4½" intervals. Solder wire tails in place to the 12-gauge wire.

4. Apply one coat of copper patina, according to the manufacturer's instructions. Allow to dry. Finish with matte spray.

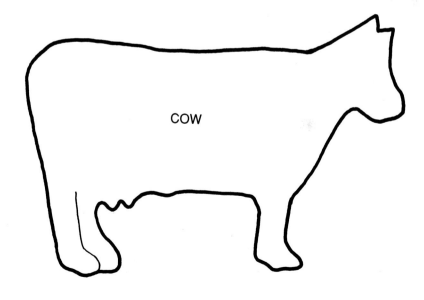

COW

Moon Leaper

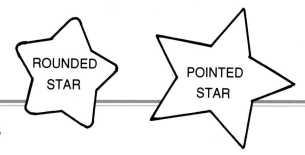

ROUNDED STAR

POINTED STAR

MATERIALS

2 feet of 14-gauge copper wire
3 feet of 18-gauge copper wire
12" square of 36-gauge tooling copper
Copper patina
Vinegar
Matte spray
Needle-nose pliers
Soldering iron and solder
Tin snips

DIRECTIONS

1. To make the wreath frame, shape the 14-gauge copper wire into a 7"-diameter circle. Twist ends firmly together and snip any excess. Set aside.

2. Transfer one cow, one moon, five rounded stars and six pointed stars onto copper. With wrong side up, place copper on a stack of paper. Emboss tail and legs on cow, according to pattern. Cut out all shapes.

3. Cut 18-gauge wire into thirteen 2½" lengths. Solder one length of wire to the center back of each star, leaving a 1" to 2" wire tail extending from each. Solder one length of wire to the back of the cow's head and

hind quarters, leaving wire tails extending. Solder the moon directly to the bottom center of the wreath.

4. Using needle-nose pliers, place the cow on the top center of the wreath by twisting wire tails around the wreath. Repeat with stars, placing on wreath as desired and varying the length of each tail; see photo. Solder each wire tail in place onto the wreath.

5. In a glass cake pan, soak the entire wreath in vinegar for three hours. Remove from vinegar and dry. Apply two coats of copper patina, according to manufacturer's instructions. Allow to dry. Finish with matte spray.

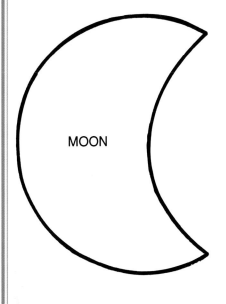

MOON

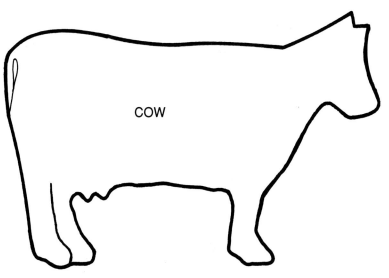

COW

Bright Light Covers

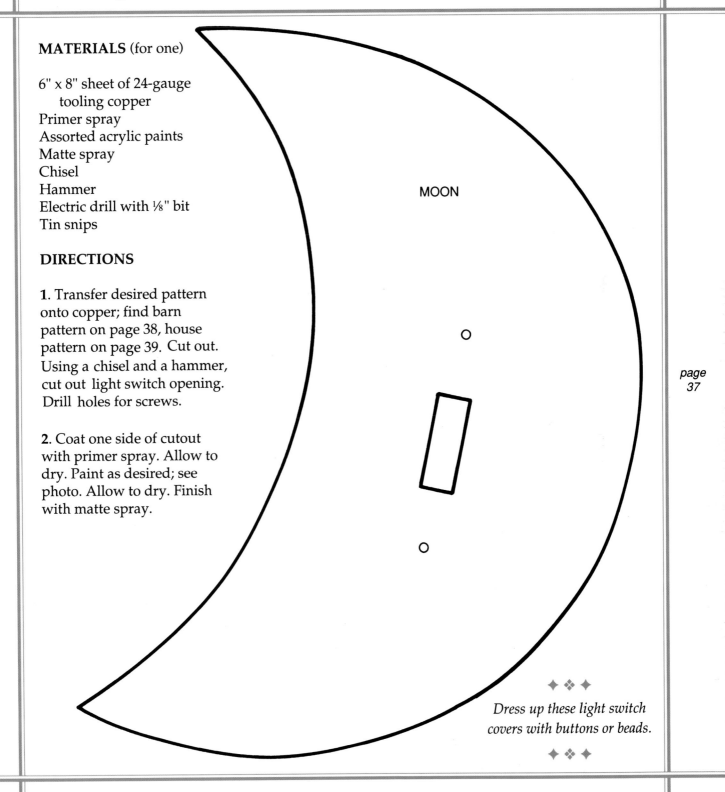

MATERIALS (for one)

6" x 8" sheet of 24-gauge
    tooling copper
Primer spray
Assorted acrylic paints
Matte spray
Chisel
Hammer
Electric drill with ⅛" bit
Tin snips

DIRECTIONS

1. Transfer desired pattern
onto copper; find barn
pattern on page 38, house
pattern on page 39. Cut out.
Using a chisel and a hammer,
cut out light switch opening.
Drill holes for screws.

2. Coat one side of cutout
with primer spray. Allow to
dry. Paint as desired; see
photo. Allow to dry. Finish
with matte spray.

MOON

*Dress up these light switch
covers with buttons or beads.*

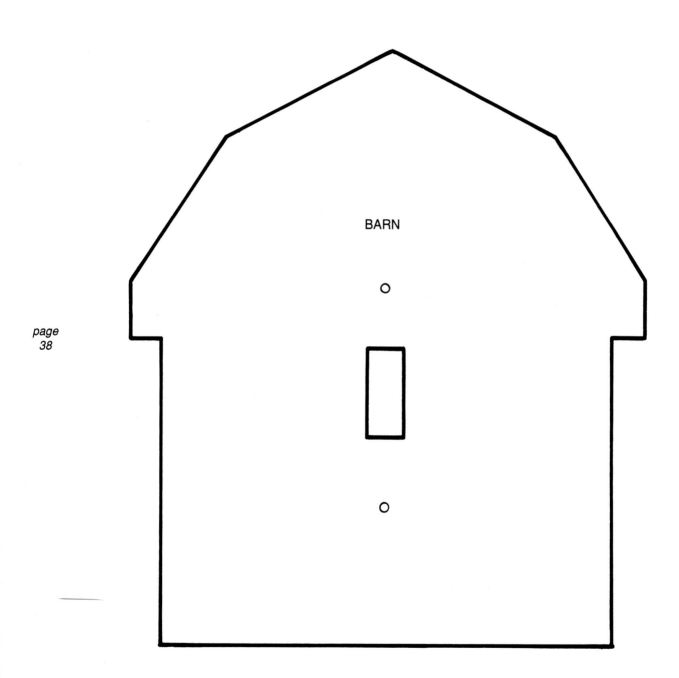

BARN

page
38

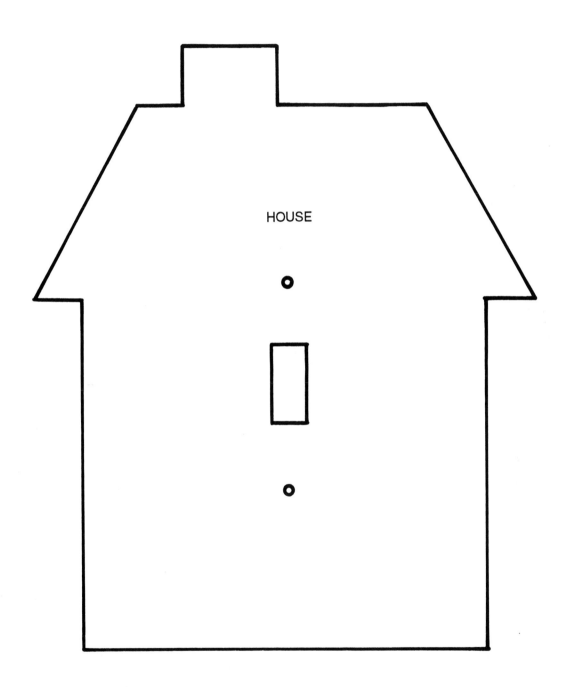

HOUSE

page 39

American Homemade

MATERIALS

20" square of 24-gauge
    tooling copper
3½ feet of 18-gauge copper
    wire
Primer spray
Acrylic paints: black, blue,
    brown, green, red,
    yellow
Matte spray
Hammer
⅛" awl
Tin snips

DIRECTIONS

1. Transfer each pattern one time onto copper. Find star and tree on page 42. Punch holes in each, according to patterns. Cut out.

2. Spray with primer. Allow to dry. Paint as desired; see photo. Finish with matte spray.

3. Cut two 8" lengths of copper wire; set remaining aside. Twist the two 8" lengths together and shape into a moon, according to pattern on page 42.

4. From remaining wire, cut four 6" lengths. Wrap one end of one wire length around bottom of moon and thread the other end through hole in top of star, twisting ends to secure. Repeat process with remaining wires, attaching house, heart and tree.

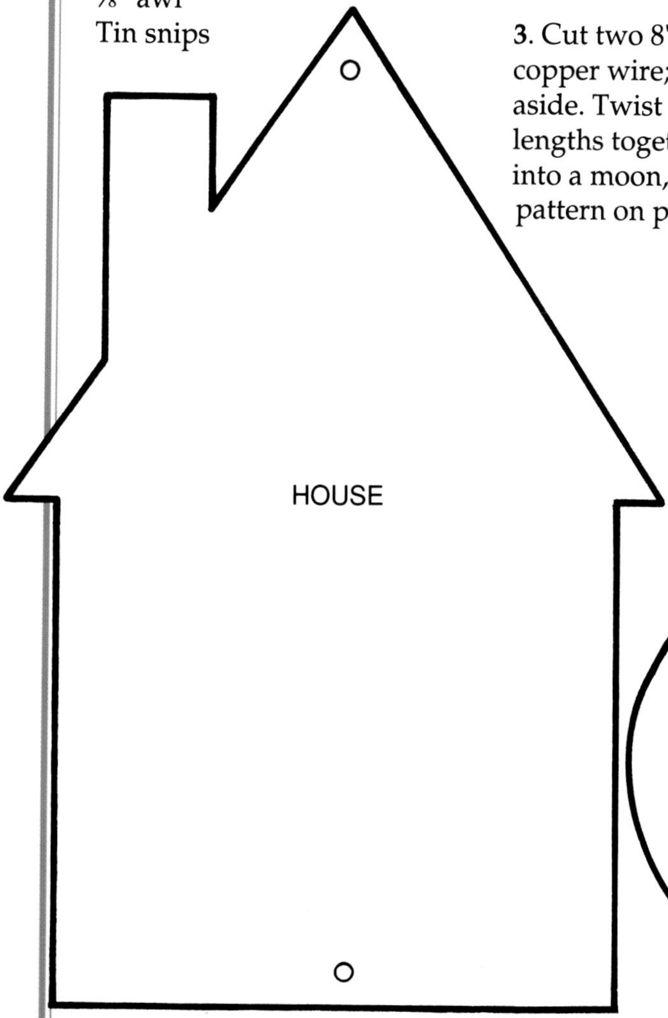

HOUSE

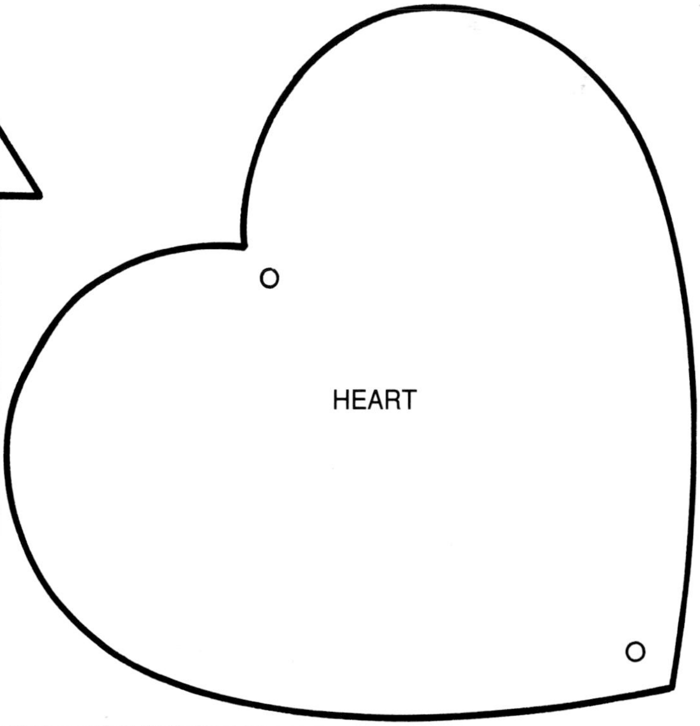

HEART

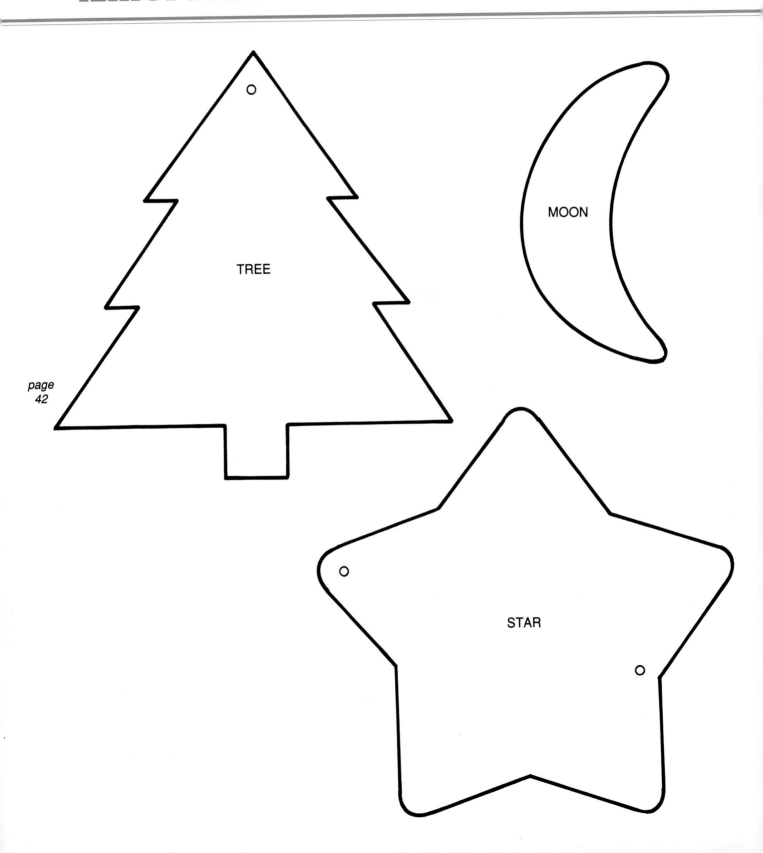

TREE

MOON

page 42

STAR

MATERIALS

9" x 15" sheet of 36-gauge
    tooling copper
7"-long ¼" dowel
Wooden base with ¼" hole
Acrylic paints, if desired
Matte spray
Super glue

DIRECTIONS

1. Transfer two fish patterns onto copper. With right side up, place copper on a stack of paper. Emboss eyes, gills and fins, according to pattern. Cut out.

2. Paint or heat-color one side of each cutout. Make sure each fish cutout is facing in the opposite direction. Finish with matte spray. Set aside.

3. Shave ½" of the dowel on one end, making it flat like a screwdriver. Put glue on wrong sides of fish. Place shaved end of dowel at center bottom of one fish. Align other cutout over dowel and fish. Glue together. Place dowel in the hole in wooden base.

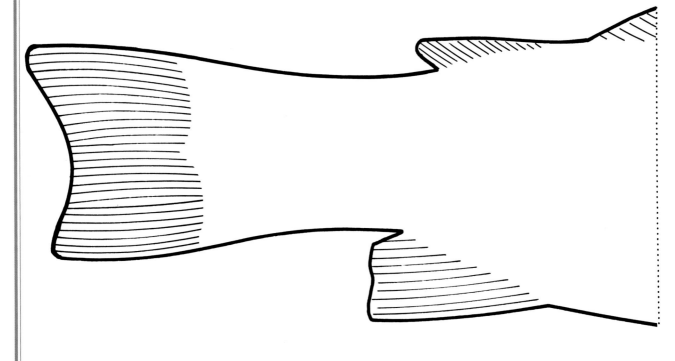

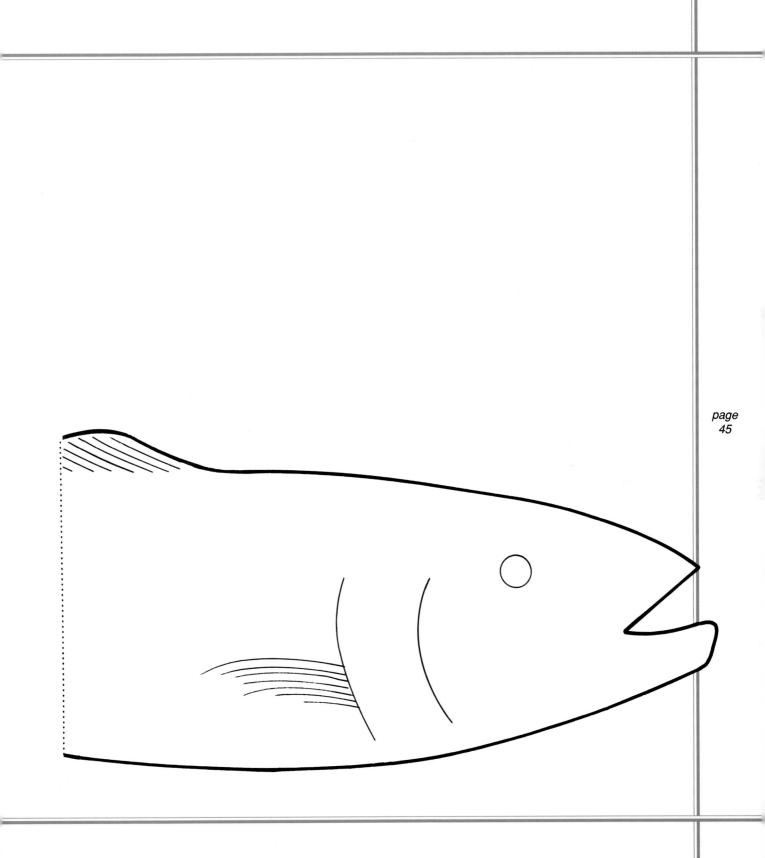

page
45

Country by Design

MATERIALS (for six)

16" x 24" sheet of 24-gauge
    tooling copper
2 feet of 20-gauge copper
    wire
Assorted acrylic paints
Matte spray
Soldering iron and solder
Tin snips

DIRECTIONS

1. Transfer each pattern one
time onto copper. Cut out.
Find more patterns on pages
50–53.

2. To make hangers, cut wire
into six 4" lengths. Bend each
length in half. Solder one
wire to the center back of
each cutout.

3. Paint as desired; see photo.
Allow to dry. Finish with
matte spray.

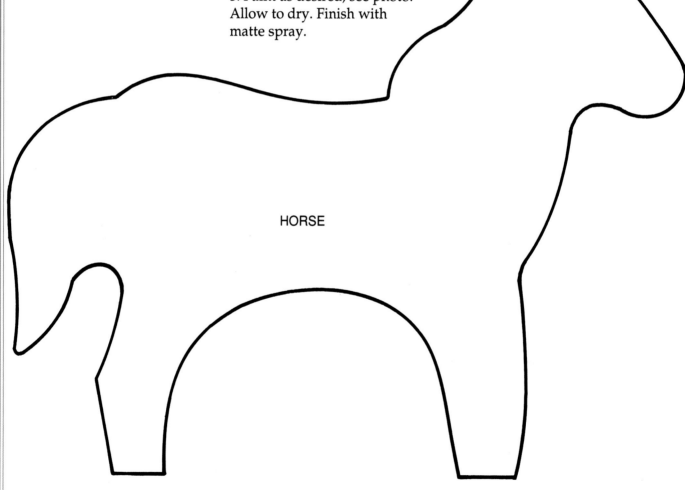

HORSE

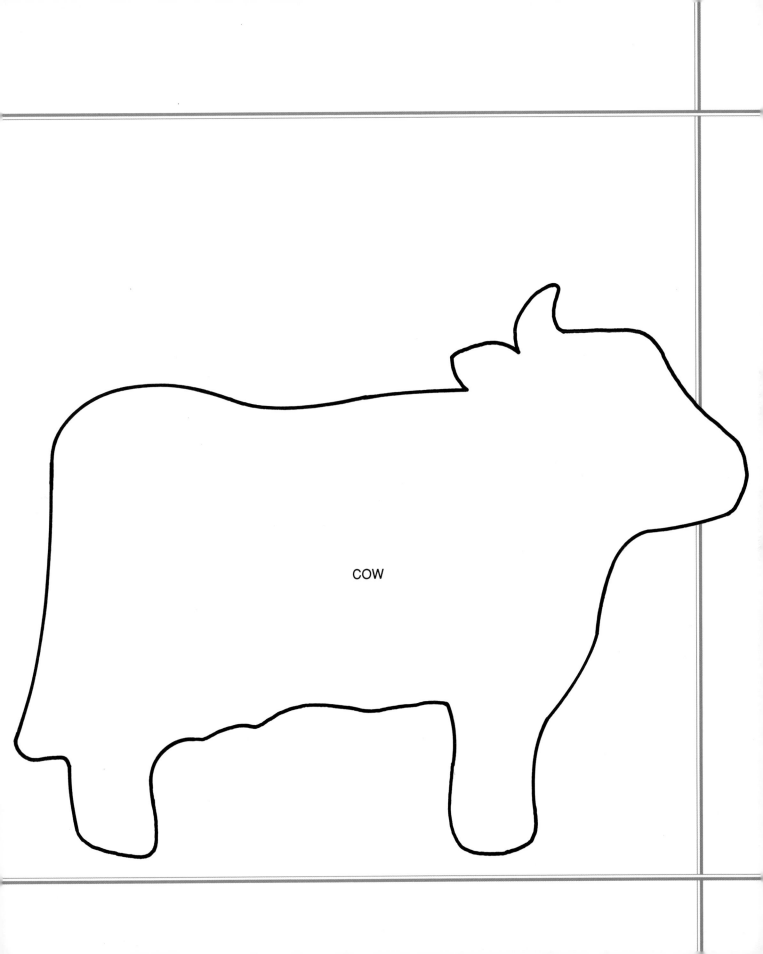

COW

*page
50*

SUN

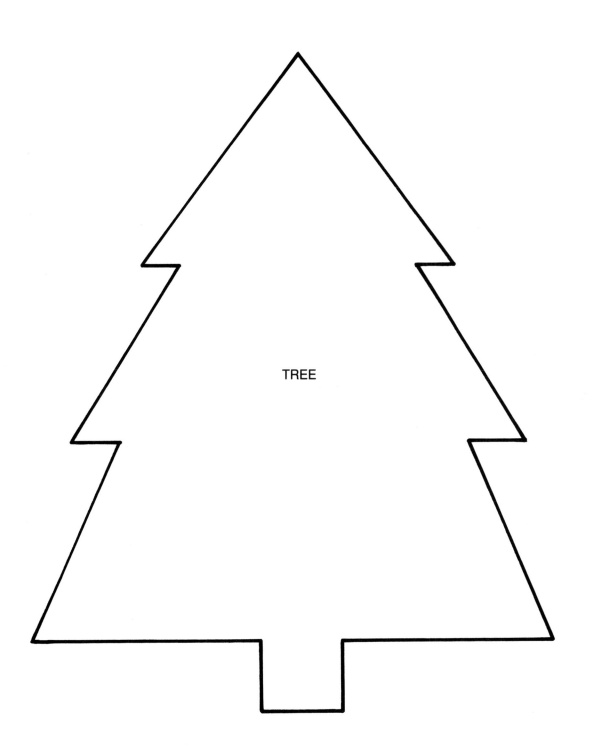

TREE

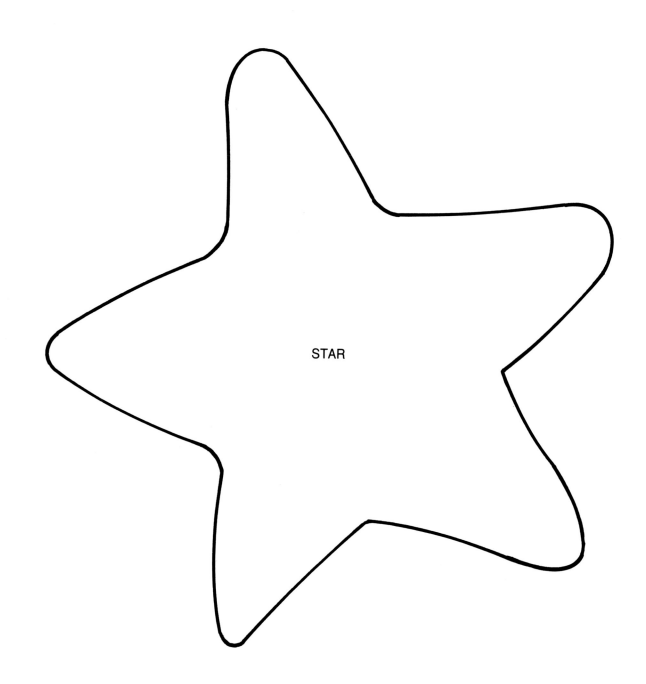

STAR

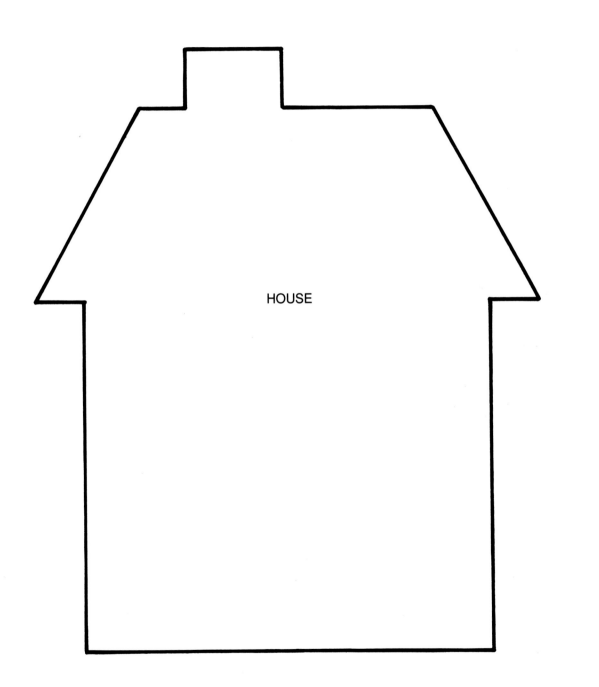

HOUSE

Dinner at 8

MATERIALS (for star)

3" square of 36-gauge tooling
    brass
6" of 10-gauge copper wire
2 feet of 32-gauge copper
    wire
2 feet of 32-gauge brass wire
Soldering iron and solder
Hammer
⅛" awl

MATERIALS (for heart)

3" square of 36-gauge tooling
    copper
6" of 10-gauge copper wire
1 foot of 18-gauge copper
    wire
2 feet of 24-gauge copper
    wire
2 feet of 32-gauge brass wire
Liver of sulphur
Hammer
⅛" awl
Soldering iron and solder

MATERIALS (for leaves)

6" square of 36-gauge tooling
    copper
Two 18" lengths of 12-gauge
    copper wire
Soldering iron and solder

DIRECTIONS (for all)

1. Transfer pattern onto
metal. With wrong side up,
place metal on a stack of
paper. Emboss according to
pattern. Turn over and using
an awl, make indentations or
holes, according to pattern.
Cut out. Set aside.

2. For star and heart, shape
the 10-gauge copper wire
into a 2"-diameter circle.
Wrap 32-gauge copper and
brass wires around 10-gauge
circle. For leaves, using
needle-nose pliers, twist the
two lengths of 12-gauge wire
together. Shape into a 2"-
diameter circle. Solder center
back of metal shape to wire
circle.

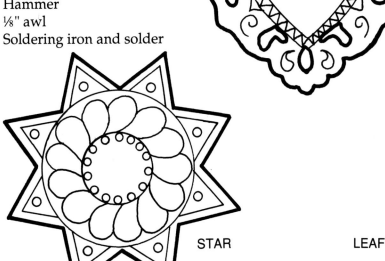

HEART

STAR

LEAF

Fancy Dinner Rose

MATERIALS (for one)

Purchased wooden napkin
    ring
3" x 12" sheet of 36-gauge
    tooling copper
10" of 24-gauge copper wire
Copper paint
Super glue
Hammer
1/16" awl
Electric drill with 1/16" drill bit

DIRECTIONS

1. Transfer one center piece, two leaves, two large petals and three small petal patterns onto copper. Place copper over a stack of paper. Punch one hole in the center of each piece according to patterns. Cut out.

2. Thread leaves onto end of wire. Thread one large petal onto wire, gluing to leaves. Repeat with remaining large petal and small petals, gluing each to the previous petal. End by threading center piece onto wire. Cut wire extending from center piece and bend in a hook at the center of the flower.

3. Shape the center piece around the bent wire end to cover it. Shape the petals to resemble a rose.

4. Drill two holes 1/4" apart in the center of the napkin ring. Paint the entire ring with copper paint. Allow to dry.

5. Thread wire extending below the rose, down through one hole in ring. Bring the wire up through the other hole and wrap several times around base of rose. Wrap remaining wire around the ring underneath the rose. Twist the end to secure.

LARGE PETAL

SMALL PETAL

CENTER PIECE

LEAF

Pumpkin Candy Cup

MATERIALS (for one)

6" square of 36-gauge
   tooling copper
Super glue
Heavy-duty craft knife

DIRECTIONS

1. Transfer cup pattern onto
copper. Transfer face pattern
on each side of cup. Using
craft knife, cut out faces.
With wrong side up, place
copper on a stack of paper.
Emboss scoring lines. Cut
out.

2. Fold on scoring lines to
shape cup. Fold tabs and
glue to the inside of the cup.

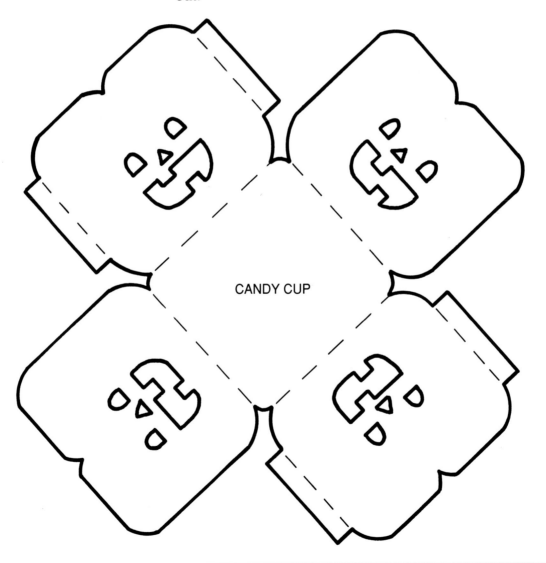

CANDY CUP

Spooky Spirits

MATERIALS

12" x 36" of 36-gauge
   tooling copper
27 feet of 14-gauge copper
   wire
27 feet of 12- gauge
   copper wire
Liver of sulphur
Soldering iron and solder

DIRECTIONS

1. Transfer one of each pattern, except bat, onto copper. Transfer bat pattern two times onto copper. Find more patterns on pages 62–64. With right side down, place copper on a stack of paper. Emboss according to patterns. Cut out each shape. Set aside.

2. Shape and wrap 12-gauge wire into a circle with a 14" diameter. Wrap 14-gauge wire around 12-gauge wire to make wreath.

3. With right side up, solder cutouts onto wire wreath as desired; see photo.

4. Apply liver of sulphur, according to manufacturer's instructions, to cutouts and wreath. Allow copper to oxidize and dry.

page 61

CAT

page
62

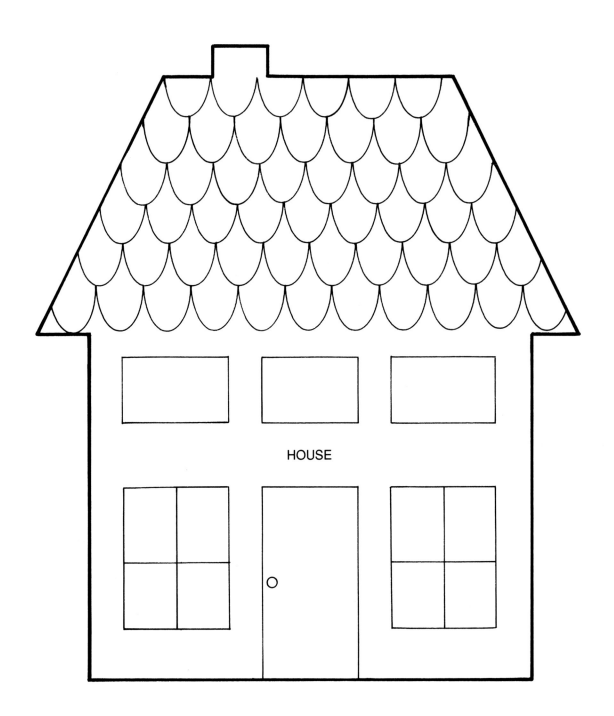

HOUSE

GHOST

BAT

page
63

WITCH

page 64

PUMPKIN

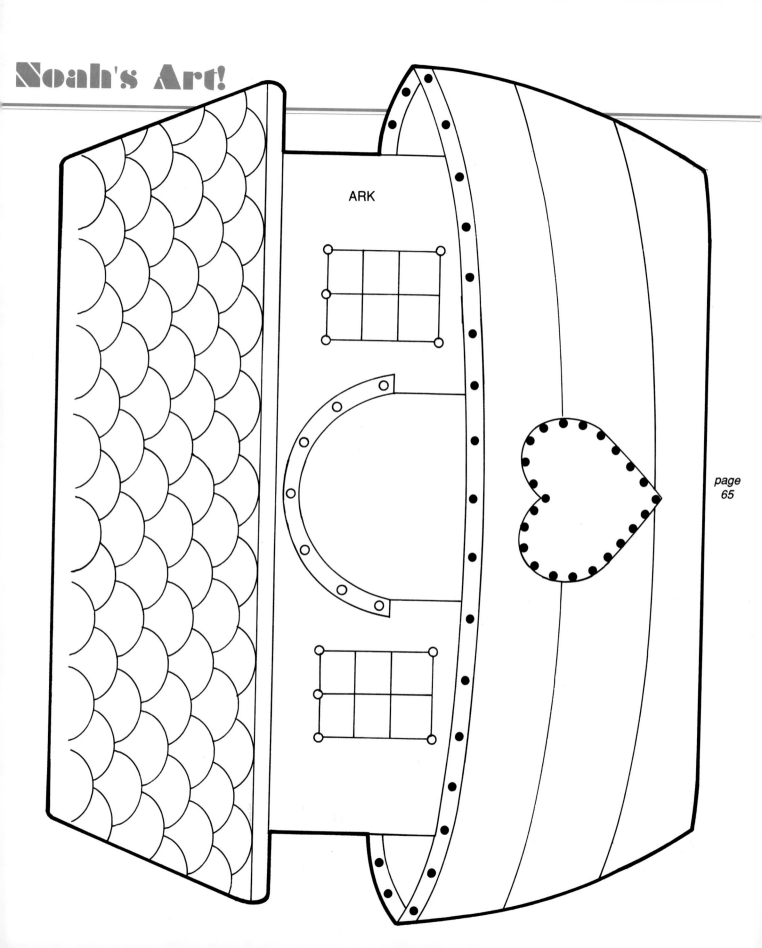

ARK

page 65

Noah's Art! continued

MATERIALS

8" x 10" sheet of 36-gauge
   tooling copper
6" square of 36-gauge tooling
   brass
2" of 32-gauge beading
   wire
Super glue
Hammer
⅛" awl

DIRECTIONS

1. Trace ark pattern on page 65. Transfer ark onto copper. With wrong side up, place copper on a stack of paper. Emboss and punch holes, according to pattern. Cut out.

2. Transfer Noah and animal patterns one time each onto brass. With wrong side up, place brass on a stack of paper. Emboss and punch holes according to patterns. Cut out.

3. Glue cutouts to right side of ark as desired. Shape beading wire into a staff and glue next to Noah.

page 67

Homestead Reflections

MATERIALS

8" x 10" mirror in a 2½"
   wooden frame
12" x 36" sheet of 18-gauge
   tooling copper
Acrylic paints: green, red,
   yellow
Matte spray
Super glue

DIRECTIONS

1. Transfer one moon, three
house, three small tree, four
large tree and ten star
patterns onto copper. Cut
out all shapes.

2. Paint house doors, roof
and windows, moon, trees
and stars as desired; see
photo. Allow to dry. Finish
cutouts with matte spray.
Allow to dry.

3. Glue cutouts to mirror
frame as desired.

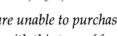

*If you are unable to purchase a
mirror with this type of frame,
have a frame shop make one for
you with your choice of stain.*

STAR

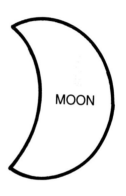

MOON

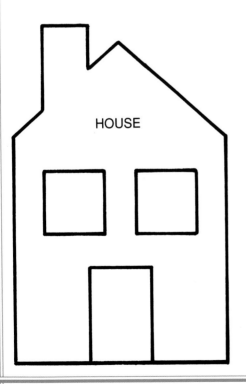

HOUSE

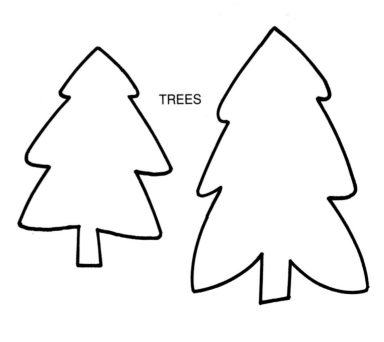

TREES

Copper Forest Wreath

MATERIALS

12" x 36" sheet of 36-gauge
    tooling copper
46" of 14-gauge copper wire
63" of 18-gauge copper wire
Copper patina
Matte spray
Needle-nose pliers
Soldering iron and solder
Tin snips

DIRECTIONS

1. Shape 14-gauge wire in a 12¼"-diameter circle. Twist ends together, snipping off excess. Set aside.

2. Transfer three large, seven medium and eleven small tree patterns onto copper. Cut out.

3. To make trunks, cut the 18-gauge wire into twenty-one 3" lengths. Solder one length of wire to the center back of each tree, leaving about a 2½" tail.

4. Using needle-nose pliers, wrap trunks onto wreath frame, varying the length of each; see photo. Position large trees first at the bottom center of the wreath.

5. Apply two coats of copper patina, according to the manufacturer's instructions. Allow to dry. Finish with matte spray.

page 71

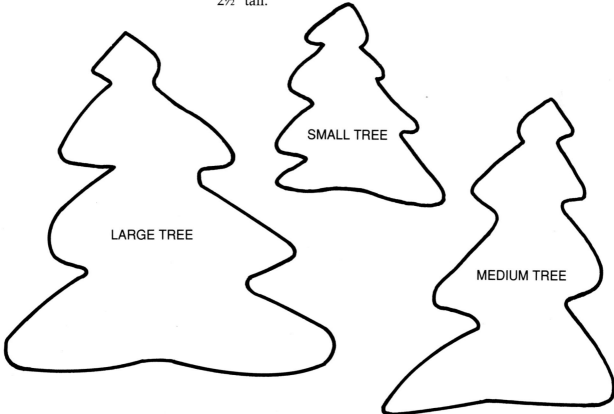

LARGE TREE

SMALL TREE

MEDIUM TREE

Extra-Special Toppers

MATERIALS (for one)

5" square of 36-gauge
    tooling brass
Standard-sized glass canning
    jar with metal lid ring

DIRECTIONS

1. Trace outside circle of metal ring onto brass.

2. With wrong side up, place brass on a stack of paper. Emboss according to pattern. Cut out circle slightly smaller than original.

3. Place embossed brass piece inside metal ring and on top of regular jar lid. Twist onto glass jar.

BRASS LID

Autumn Leaves

MATERIALS

16" of 10-gauge copper wire
9 feet of 18-gauge copper
    wire
40" of 24-gauge copper wire
12" x 30" sheet of 36-gauge
    tooling copper
Copper paint
Needle-nose pliers
Soldering iron and solder
Tin snips

DIRECTIONS

1. Shape 10-gauge wire into a branch. Set aside.

2. Transfer six each of pattern A, five each of patterns B and C and two each of pattern D onto copper. Find more leaf patterns on page 76.

3. With wrong side up, place copper on a stack of paper. Emboss veins according to patterns. Cut out leaves.

4. Heat-color leaves until desired colors are achieved. Do not overheat leaves or colors will be lost.

5. To make stems, cut 18-gauge wire into eighteen 6" lengths. Solder one length of wire to the center back of each leaf, leaving wire tail extending.

6. Using needle-nose pliers, wrap stems around wire branch, varying the length of each stem; see photo. Solder each stem in place to the wire branch. Cover soldering spots with copper paint. Allow to dry.

7. To make spirals, cut 24-gauge wire into five 8" lengths. Wrap each length around a pencil to coil and gently pull to stretch. Wrap onto branch as desired.

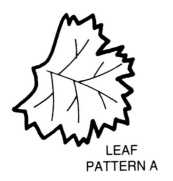

LEAF
PATTERN A

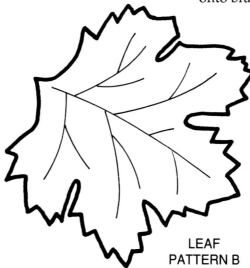

LEAF
PATTERN B

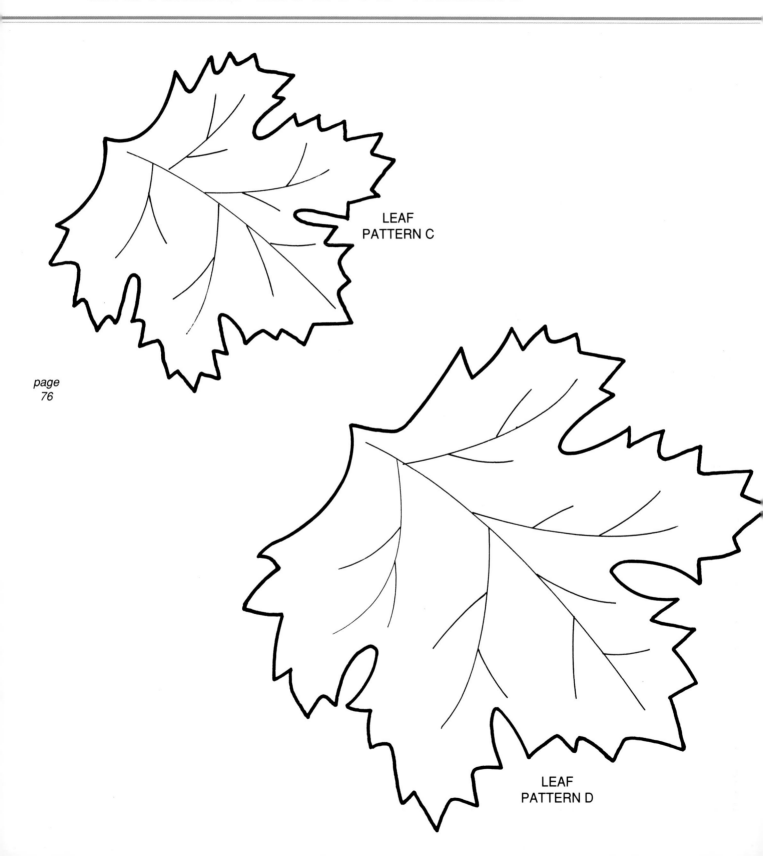

LEAF
PATTERN C

*page
76*

LEAF
PATTERN D

Flickering Night Lights

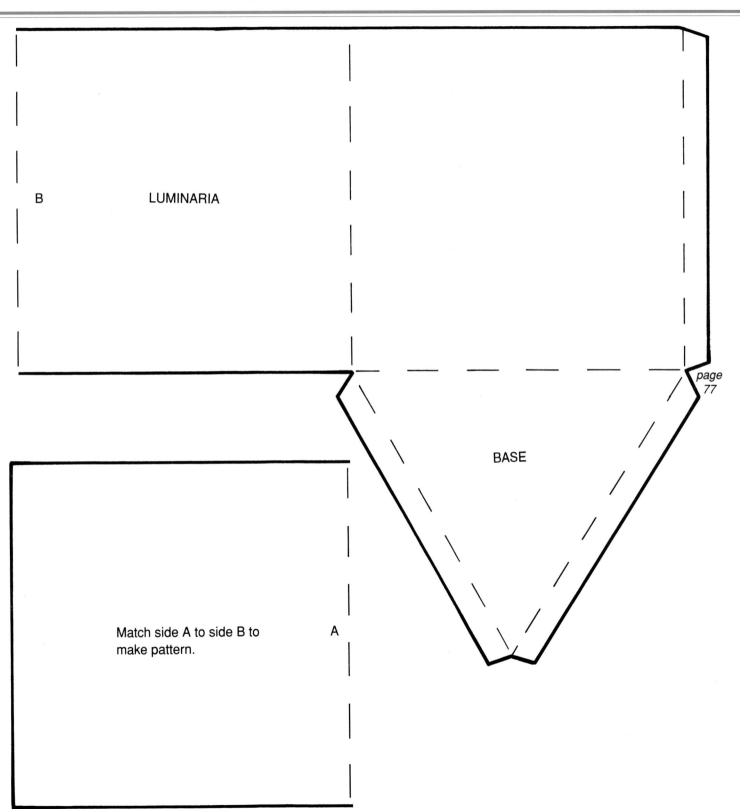

B   LUMINARIA

page 77

BASE

Match side A to side B to make pattern.

A

MATERIALS (for three)

12" x 36" sheet of 36-gauge
    tooling copper
Three votive candles
Super glue
Hammer
¹⁄₁₆" awl

DIRECTIONS

1. Transfer luminaria pattern on page 77 three times onto copper. With right side up, place copper on a stack of paper. Punch holes of one star, sun or moon pattern onto each side panel of each luminaria; see photo. Turn over; emboss scoring lines on each. Cut out.

2. To make luminarias, fold in on scoring lines. Glue bottom tabs and side tab inside luminaria.

3. Heat-color to achieve desired highlights. Place candles inside luminarias. Do not place lighted candles on flammable surfaces.

STAR

SUN

MOON

Prairie Luminarias

MATERIALS (for two)

12" x 36" sheet of 36-gauge
   tooling copper
Three votive candles
Super glue
Hammer
⅛" awl
Heavy-duty craft knife

DIRECTIONS

1. Enlarge and transfer roof pattern on page 82 onto copper. With right side up, place copper on a stack of paper. Punch holes according to moon pattern on one roof panel. Turn copper over and emboss scoring lines. Using craft knife, cut out one star on remaining roof panels. Cut out roof.

2. Fold roof in on scoring lines. Glue front of tab to back of open roof edge.

3. From copper, cut one 5" x 20½" sheet. With sheet lengthwise, emboss sheet with vertical scoring lines at 5" intervals. Transfer house pattern on page 83 to each 5" section. Using craft knife, cut out windows. Place on stack of paper and punch holes, according to tree pattern on house.

4. To make house, fold sheet on all vertical lines. Glue front of ½" x 5" tab to back of open house edge. Place candles inside houses. Place roofs on houses. Do not place lighted candles on flammable surfaces.

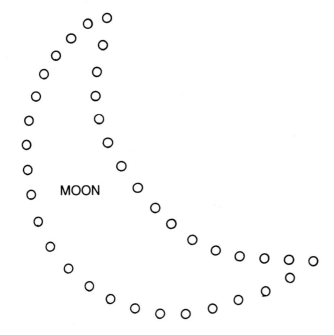

MOON

STAR

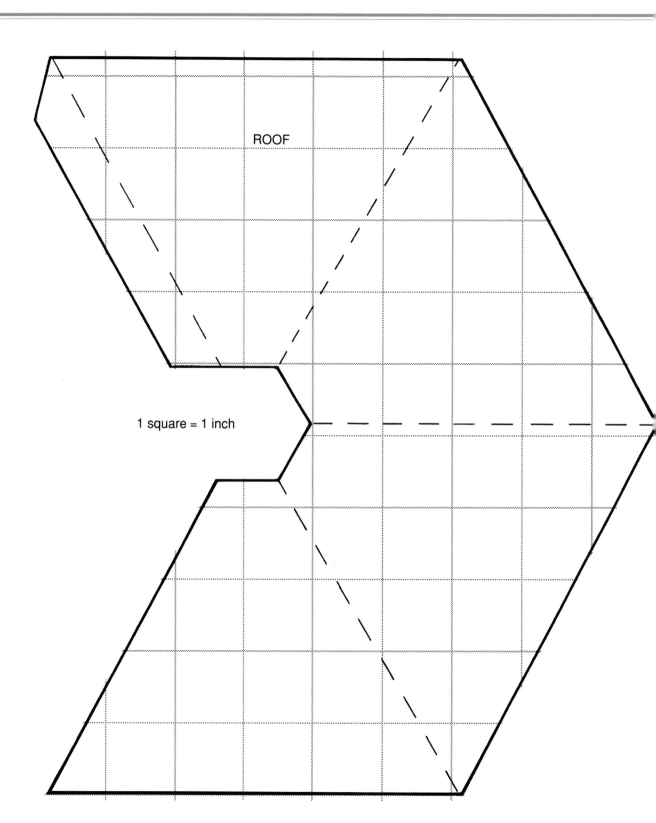

ROOF

page
82

1 square = 1 inch

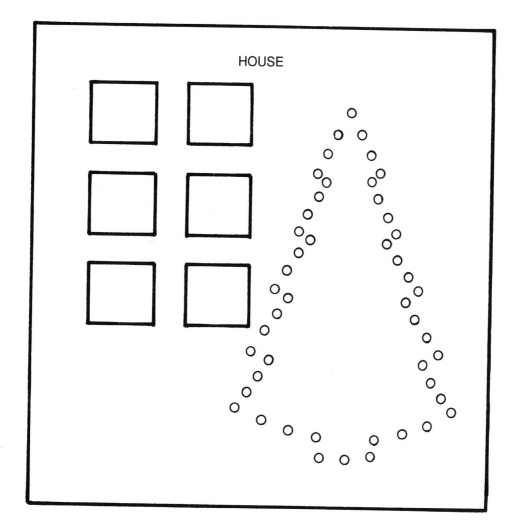

HOUSE

Dandy Dude Boots

MATERIALS (for rose boot)

3" x 5" sheet of 36-gauge
   tooling copper
30-40 red seed beads
Acrylic paints: green, mauve,
   red, white
6" of copper colored string
Super glue
Hammer
1/16" awl

DIRECTIONS

1. Transfer boot pattern onto copper. Find more patterns on page 86. With right side up, place brass on a stack of paper. Emboss according to pattern. Cut out.

2. Paint heart, leaves and rose according to embossed pattern. Allow to dry. To decorate boot, glue seed beads as desired.

3. Punch hole in center top of boot. To make a hanger, thread the string through the hole and tie the ends together.

◆ ❖ ◆

Make a collection of boots out of aluminum, brass and copper. See photo and patterns for other painting and embossing ideas.

◆ ❖ ◆

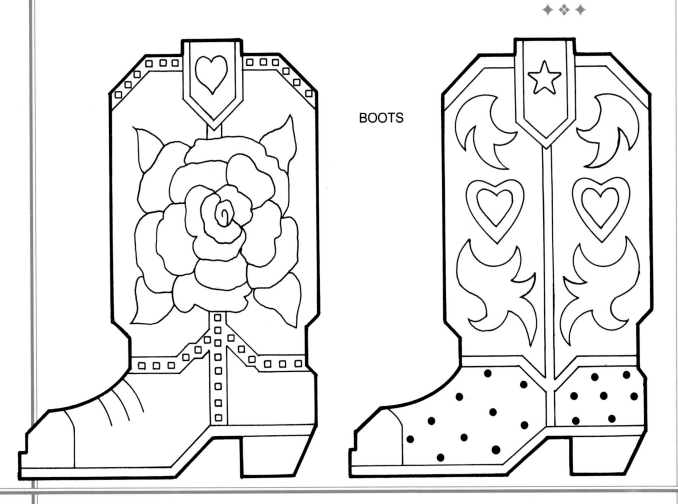

BOOTS

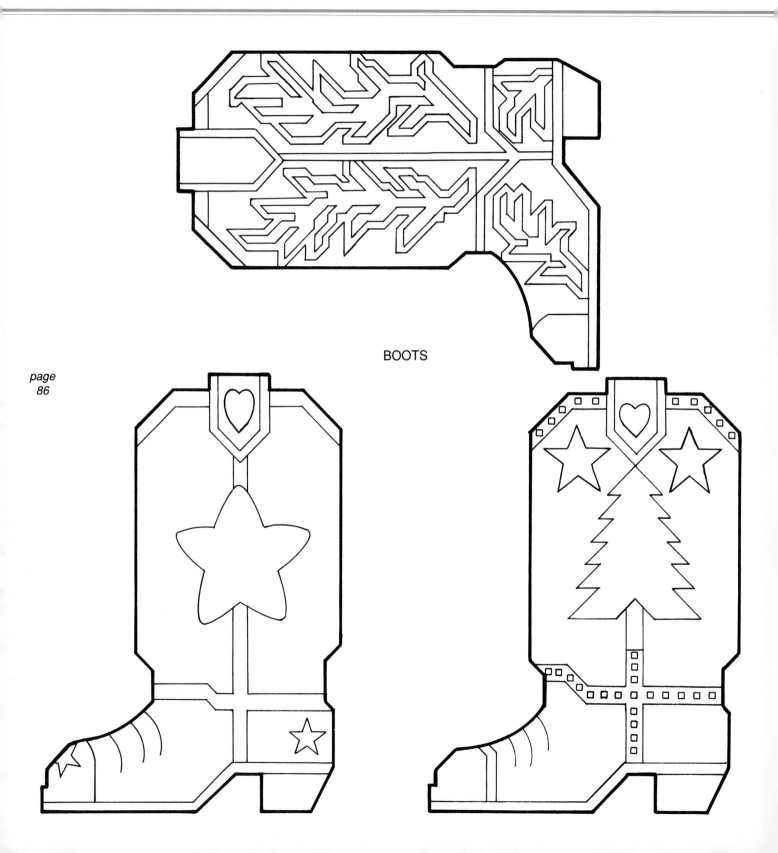

BOOTS

page 86

MATERIALS

10" x 12" sheet of 24-gauge
    tooling copper
5" of 14-gauge copper wire
Copper patina
Matte spray
Vinegar
Soldering iron and solder
Tin snips

DIRECTIONS

1. Transfer reindeer pattern onto copper and cut out.

2. To make hanger, bend the length of copper wire in half. Solder each end of the wire to the center back of the reindeer.

3. In a glass cake pan, soak the reindeer in vinegar for three hours. Remove from vinegar and dry. Apply two coats of copper patina, according to manufacturer's instructions. Allow to dry; finish with matte spray.

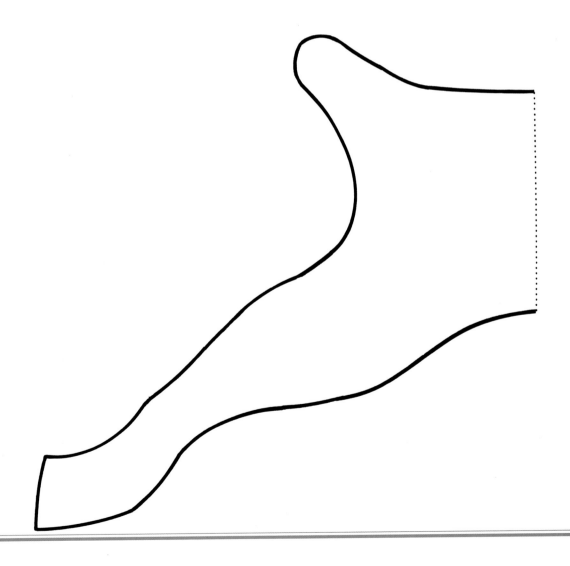

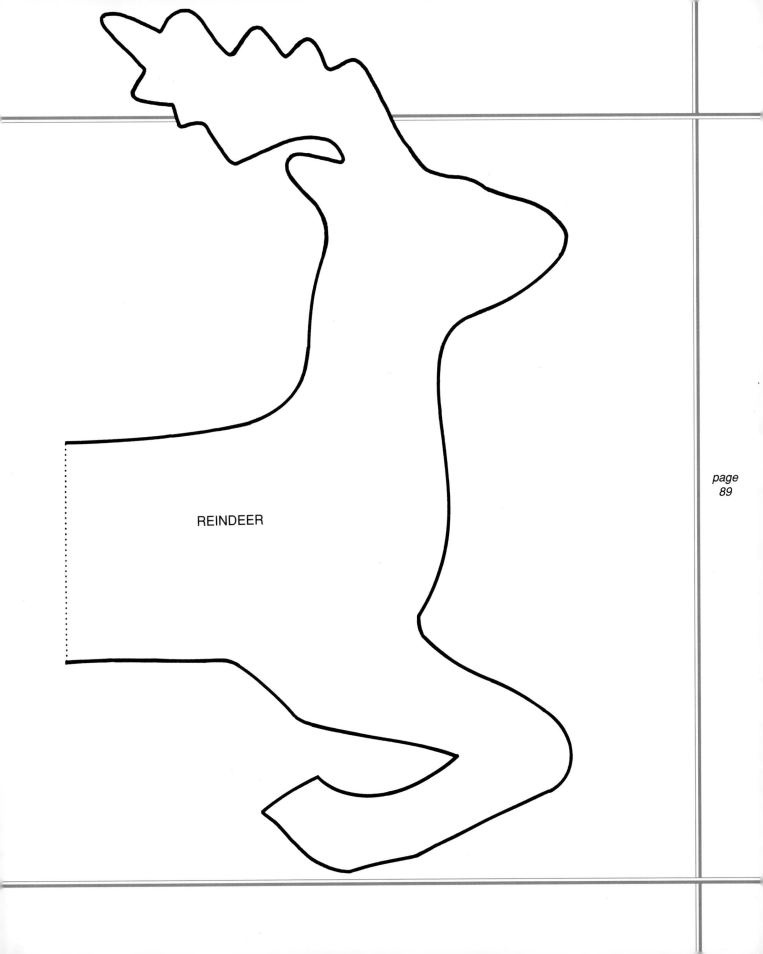

REINDEER

Host of Angels

MATERIALS (for one)

12" square of 36-gauge
    tooling brass
Primer spray
Assorted acrylic paints
Matte spray

DIRECTIONS

1. Transfer angel pattern onto
brass and cut out. Find more
angel patterns on pages 92
and 94.

2. Spray front side of angel
with primer. Allow to dry.

3. Paint angel as desired; see
photos on pages 2, 6, 90, 93
and 95 for ideas. Allow to
dry. Finish with matte spray.

✦ ❖ ✦

*Use a copy machine to reduce
or enlarge the patterns and
make a host of angels from
very large to very small.
Trumpeter angels may also be
flipped to face either direction.*

✦ ❖ ✦

ANGEL

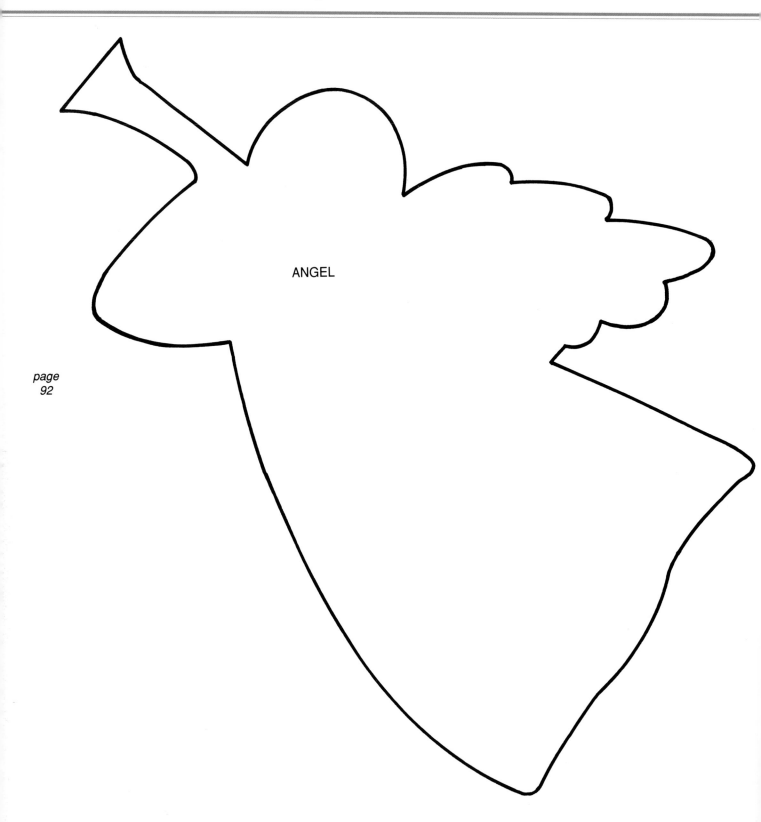

ANGEL

page
92

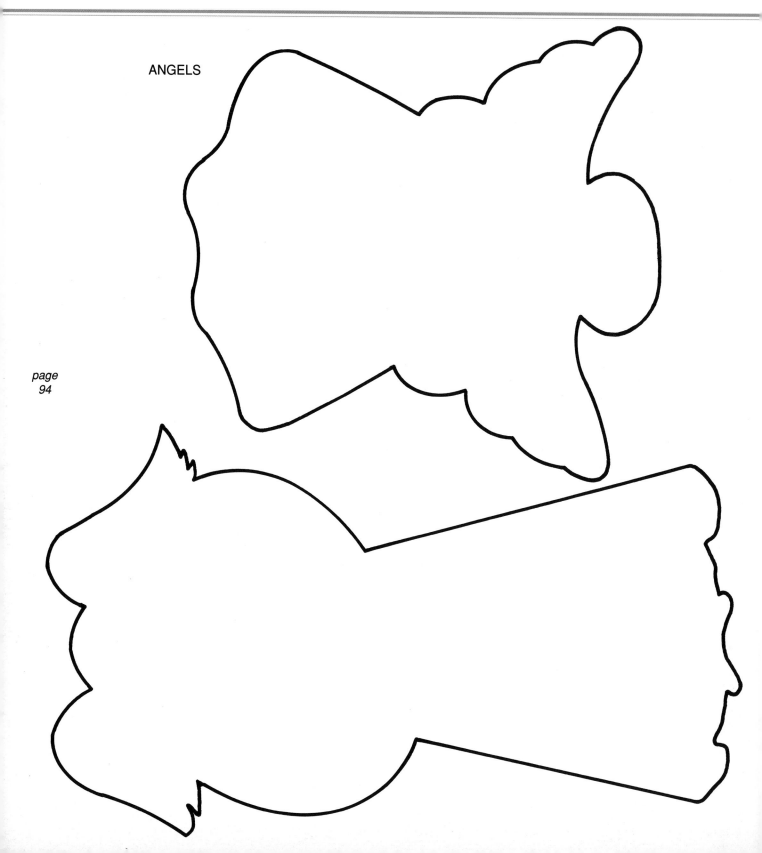

ANGELS

page
94

Clinging Vine Topiaries

MATERIALS (for each)

Two ⁷/₁₆" bare bronze
   welding rods, 3 feet each
6" of 24-gauge copper wire
14" of 14-gauge copper wire
1 foot of 10-gauge copper
   wire
Soldering iron and solder

DIRECTIONS

1. Make a paper pattern for a 7" x 11" heart, an 8" x 9" tapered tree or an 8" five-point star.

2. Bend one welding rod into desired shape for heart, tree or star. Wrap the ends with 24-gauge wire to secure. Bend second welding rod into same shape, but make it slightly smaller than the first with 1½" tails extending from the bottom. These tails will become the stands for the topiary. For a star, bend both welding rods the same size and use the 10-gauge copper wire for the stand.

3. Solder the wire wrapped ends together.

4. Bend the 14-gauge copper wire in a heart or star to top your topiary. Attach shape to top of topiary with 24-gauge wire and solder to secure.

✦ ❖ ✦

If you prefer, make one of the beaded ornaments on page 99 to place on top of your topiary as we have. See photo for ideas.

✦ ❖ ✦

page 97

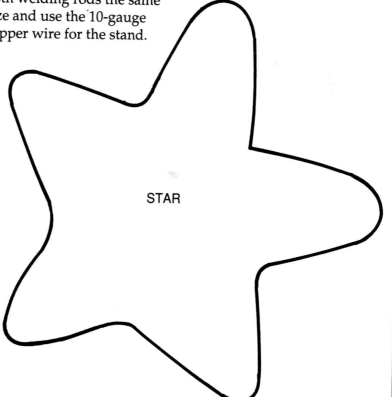

STAR

Beaded Ornaments

MATERIALS (for one)

17½" of 18-gauge
    copper wire
3 feet of 24-gauge
    copper wire
3 feet of 36-gauge
    copper wire
Fourteen assorted beads
Tin snips

DIRECTIONS (for star)

1. Cut one 15" length of 18-gauge wire; set remaining aside. Using pattern as a guide, shape wire into a star. Twist ends together and snip excess wire. Find star on page 97.

2. Wrap 24-gauge wire around star, adding five–seven beads at random. Twist ends and snip any excess. Repeat with 36-gauge wire, adding remaining beads.

3. Shape remaining 18-gauge wire into a two-sided hook. Hang one end on star ornament and squeeze to close.

✦ ❖ ✦

For additional ornaments, follow the above instructions, using the heart and tree patterns.

✦ ❖ ✦

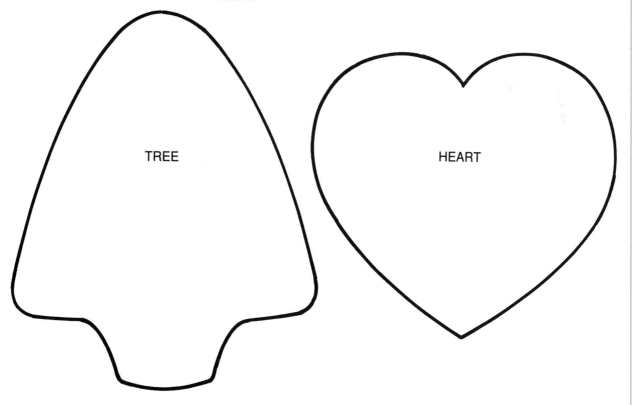

TREE

HEART

Sweet Angela

MATERIALS

8½" x 11" piece of mat board
8" square of 36-gauge
    tooling brass
4" of 24-gauge brass wire
Three jewelry pins
Five 1" brass jewelry accents
Brass heart jewelry accent
1¼ yards of ¼" silk ribbon
Assorted acrylic paints
Hammer
¹⁄₁₆ " awl

◆ ❖ ◆

*Pull the ribbon and watch this
sweet angel's wings move!*

◆ ❖ ◆

DIRECTIONS

1. Transfer one body, one apron and two wing patterns on page 102 onto mat board. Cut out. Transfer wings, sleeve edging and apron edging patterns on page 103 onto brass. With wrong side up, place brass on a stack of paper. Emboss according to patterns. Cut out. Set aside.

2. Using the mat board cutouts, paint the face, dress and apron, according to patterns and with desired colors. Allow to dry. Glue brass wing cutouts over the corresponding mat board wings. Glue the brass sleeve edging to the mat board sleeves. Glue the brass apron edging to the mat board apron. Glue the five jewelry accents along the bottom of the dress.

3. Using an awl, punch holes in the mat board wings and body according to pattern. Put one pin in the hole at the neck, with the head of the pin facing the front of the body. Snip off tip of pin and twist to form a loop. Place the remaining two pins into the holes on the body with the head of pins facing the front of the body. Next, put the pins through the inner holes on each wing. Snip the tips and twist ends into flat spirals. These will act as joints to allow the wings to move.

4. Using a needle and thread, run thread several times through outer holes on wings. Stitch loosely so the wings will move. Cut the thread and tie the ends together.

5. Center and glue the apron piece over the body piece.

6. Cut the silk ribbon into a 15" length and a 30" length. To make the hanger, tie the ends of the 15" length around the wire loop at the neck of the angel. To make the pull that will move the wings, loop the 30" length around the thread at the back of the wings. Tie the heart charm a few inches from the ends of the ribbon.

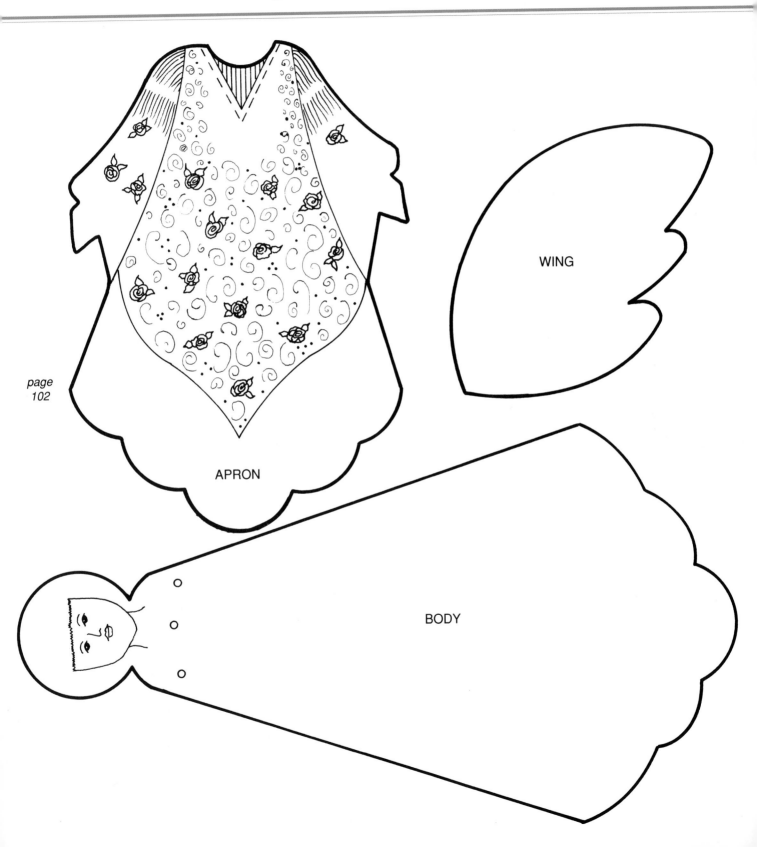

page 102

APRON

WING

BODY

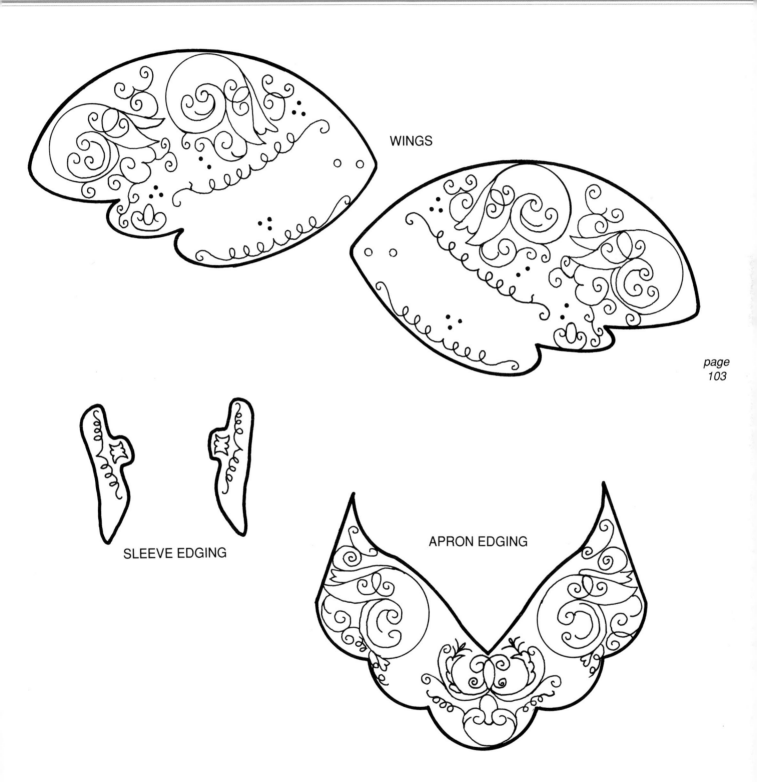

WINGS

page
103

SLEEVE EDGING

APRON EDGING

Western Wire Trees

MATERIALS (for large tree)

5½ feet of 14-gauge copper wire
15 feet of 32-gauge copper wire
6" square of 36-gauge tooling copper
Primer spray
Acrylic paints: blue, brown, green, peach , red, white, yellow
Hammer
1⁄16" awl

DIRECTIONS

1. Shape 14-gauge wire into one large tree according to pattern on page 107. Make crisscross pattern on tree with 14-gauge wire. Wrap tree with 32-gauge wire.

2. Coat tree with primer spray. Allow to dry. Paint tree green. Set aside and allow to dry.

3. Transfer three each: angel, large flower, large heart and large star patterns onto copper. Cut out all shapes.

4. Coat ornaments with primer spray. Allow to dry. Paint ornaments as desired. Allow to dry. To antique, wash all ornaments with brown paint; remove excess. Allow to dry.

5. Punch one hole in top of each ornament and thread with a short length of 32-gauge wire. Place ornaments on tree, twisting wire to secure.

✦ ❖ ✦

For an additional tree, follow the above instructions, using the small tree pattern and two each of the small ornament patterns.

✦ ❖ ✦

LARGE STAR

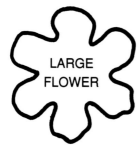
LARGE FLOWER

LARGE HEART

BELL

SMALL HEART

SMALL FLOWER

ANGEL

SMALL STAR

page
106

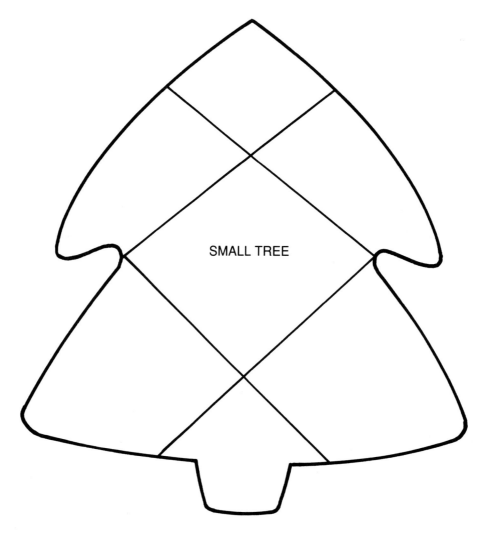

SMALL TREE

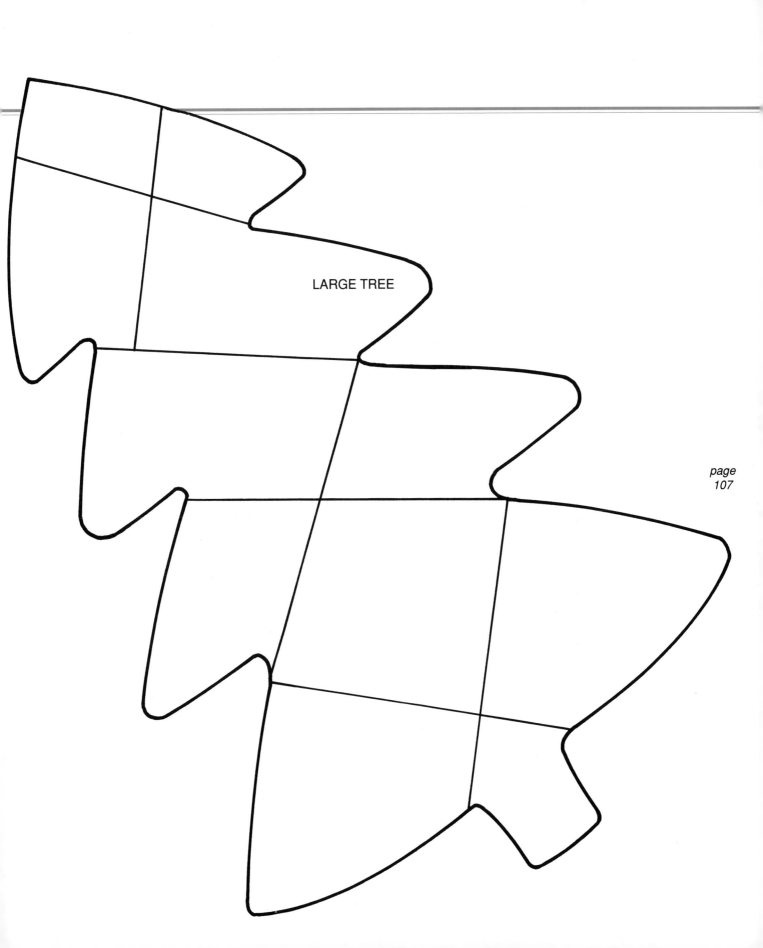

LARGE TREE

page
107

Copper Critter Fence

MATERIALS

One purchased 14" tree
    with stand
8" x 12" sheet of 36-gauge
    tooling copper
Super glue
Heavy-duty craft knife

DIRECTIONS

1. Transfer fence pattern four times onto copper. Cut out four sections. Using craft knife, cut out area between fence posts.

2. Bend fence post after squirrel on one fence piece. Glue this post to straight ends of another fence post before bird. Repeat with remaining fence pieces, aligning to make a square. Place tree inside fence.

Festive Garland

MATERIALS (for tree)

12" square of 36-gauge
    tooling copper
54" of 14-gauge copper
    wire
75" of 24-gauge copper
    wire
Copper paint
Matte spray
Needle-nose pliers
Soldering iron and solder

DIRECTIONS

1. Transfer tree pattern twenty-five times onto copper. Cut out.

2. To make stems, cut the 24-gauge wire into twenty-five 3" lengths. Solder one length of wire to the center back of each tree, leaving wire tail. If needed, polish the front of the trees with steel wool to remove tarnish where soldered.

3. Lay the 14-gauge wire out straight. Using needle-nosed pliers, wrap each stem onto 14-gauge wire at 2" intervals. Vary the length of each stem; see photo. Solder each stem in place to the 14-gauge wire. Cover soldering spots with copper paint. Finish with matte spray.

✦ ❖ ✦

For an additional garland, follow the above instructions, using the bear pattern.

✦ ❖ ✦

TREE

BEAR

Embossed Evergreen

MATERIALS

12" x 15" sheet of 24-gauge
    tooling copper
10" x 12" sheet of 36-gauge
    tooling brass
8" square of 36-gauge
    tooling copper
16" of 24-gauge copper wire
1 yard of gold braid
Super glue
Soldering iron and solder
Tin snips
Scissors

DIRECTIONS

1. Enlarge and transfer large triangle pattern onto 24-gauge copper. Cut out. Enlarge and transfer small triangle pattern onto brass. With wrong side up, place brass on a stack of paper. Emboss triangle according to pattern on page 114. Cut out. Transfer eight bird patterns on page 114 onto brass. Emboss and cut out. Transfer eight wing patterns onto 36-gauge copper. Emboss and cut out.

2. With right side up, place small triangle over large triangle. Glue together, leaving a 1" copper border at sides and bottom and a 2" copper border at top.

3. Glue gold braid around outline of small triangle. Glue wings onto birds, four facing to the right and four facing to the left. Glue three of the left facing birds at the top right of the small triangle. Glue three right facing birds at the top left of the small triangle. Glue the remaining two birds facing each other, at the base of the small triangle; see photo.

4. To make hanger, bend copper wire in half. Solder ends to back center of tree.

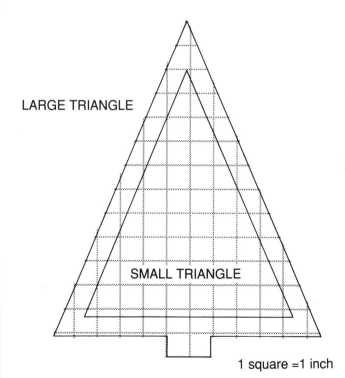

LARGE TRIANGLE

SMALL TRIANGLE

1 square =1 inch

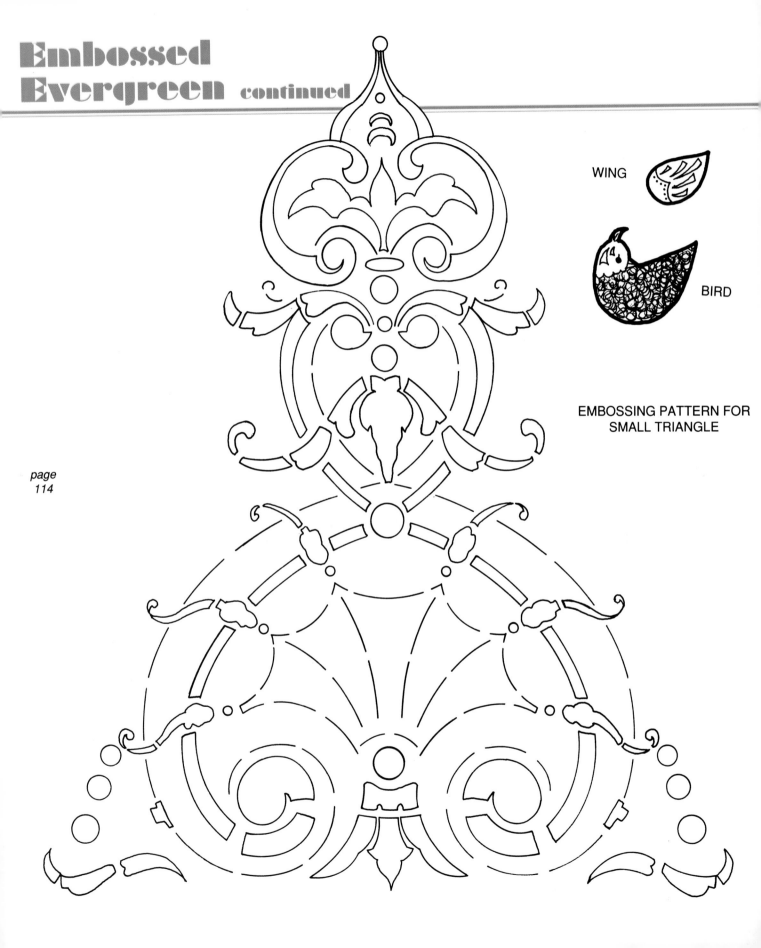

Embossed Evergreen continued

WING

BIRD

EMBOSSING PATTERN FOR
SMALL TRIANGLE

*page
114*

Holiday Plant Markers

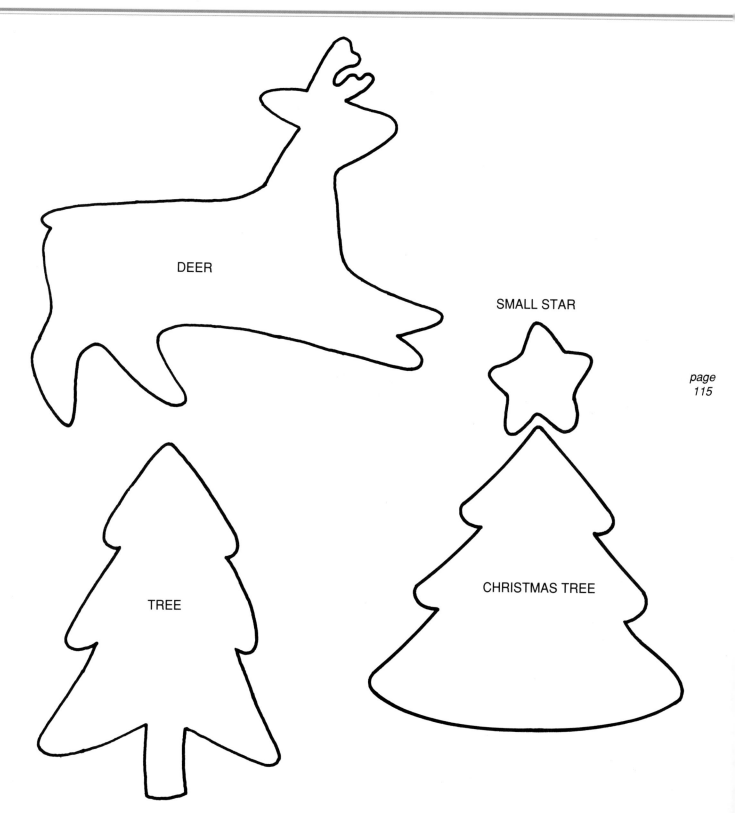

DEER

SMALL STAR

page
115

TREE

CHRISTMAS TREE

MATERIALS (for five)

3" x 12" sheet of 36-gauge
   tooling copper
30" of 18-gauge copper wire
Acrylic paints: black, blue,
   green, red, yellow
Copper patina
Matte spray
Soldering iron and solder
Tin snips

DIRECTIONS

1. Transfer each pattern one
time onto copper. Cut out.
Find more patterns on page
115.

2. Solder small star to top of
Christmas tree. Cut five 6"
lengths of 18-gauge wire.
Solder one wire to center
back of each cutout.

3. Antique cutouts with
copper patina or paint them
as desired; see photo. Allow
to dry. Finish with matte
spray.

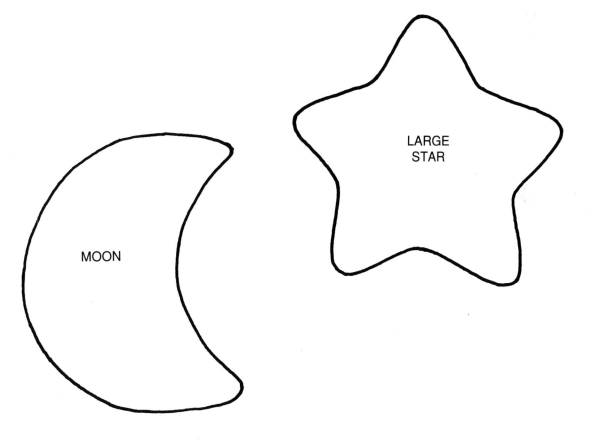

MOON

LARGE
STAR

Pine Forest Deer

MATERIALS (for two)

8" x 8" sheet of 36-gauge
    tooling brass
14" of metallic gold thread
Hammer
1/16" awl

DIRECTIONS

1. Transfer deer pattern two
times onto brass. Cut out.

2. With right side up, place
deer on a stack of paper.
Punch two holes for hanger
according to pattern.

3. Cut thread into two 7"
lengths. To make hanger,
thread one length through
both holes on one deer and
tie ends together. Repeat on
remaining deer with
remaining length of thread.

DEER

Cookie-Cutter Centerpieces

MATERIALS (for tree)

One 2" star cookie-cutter
One 5" tin Christmas tree
    cookie-cutter
5"-wide clay flowerpot and
    saucer
24-ounce plastic tumbler
Two to three cups of plaster
    of paris
4" piece of ¼" dowel
Dark green acrylic paint
Copper paint
Sheet moss
Dried cranberries
Miniature pinecones
Heavy-duty craft knife
Small nail
Hammer
Hot glue gun and glue stick

DIRECTIONS

1. Mix the plaster of paris according to manufacturer's instructions. Pour into tumbler; insert dowel. Allow to set. Using craft knife, trim the tumbler to ¼" above the plaster of paris. Insert the tumbler in the flowerpot.

2. Using green and copper paint, sponge-paint extended part of dowel, flowerpot and saucer. Allow to dry. Glue saucer to bottom of flowerpot. Glue moss to the plaster of paris, mounding at top of flowerpot. Add cranberries and pinecones as desired; see photo.

3. To age cookie-cutters, soak in water overnight. Center and nail bottom of tree cookie-cutter to dowel. Glue star cookie-cutter to top of tree; see photo.

◆ ❖ ◆

For an additional centerpiece, follow the above instructions, using one 2" gingerbread man cookie-cutter and two miniature cookie-cutters. Using a ⅛" awl, punch a hole in the gingerbread man's arm and wire on the miniature cookie-cutters; see photo.

◆ ❖ ◆

Golden Rose Ball

MATERIALS (for two)

Four spools (24 yards) of
    32-gauge beading wire
Two round balloons
48" of 2" gold mesh wire
Copper spray paint
Matte spray

DIRECTIONS

1. Inflate balloons to 5"
diameter.

2. Wrap two spools of
beading wire around each
balloon, reserving 6" from
one spool. Coat generously
with matte spray. Allow to
dry.

3. Pop balloon and gently
remove from center of
ornament. To make hanger,
cut 6" of beading wire in half.
Tie one length of beading
wire at the top of each
ornament.

4. To make roses and leaves,
cut the gold mesh wire into
three 6" lengths, three 5"
lengths and five 3" lengths.
Then cut the lengths in half
horizontally.

5. Use 6" lengths and 5"
lengths to make twelve roses.
Fold ribbon in half
lengthwise. Twist and roll
one short end to make rose
center; see Diagram A.
Continue twisting and
rolling long free tail around
center to complete; see
Diagram B. Stitch at bottom
to secure. If some petals look
out of place or start to unfurl,
stitch with needle and thread
to secure.

Diagram A

Diagram B

6. Use 3" lengths to make ten
leaves. With one ribbon
length, fold ends diagonally
across to center and down;
see Diagram C. Fold sides
across and down again to
make leaf shape; see
Diagram D. Stitch leaf at
bottom to secure.

Diagram C

Diagram D

7. Lightly spray roses and
leaves with copper paint.
Glue to top of ornaments as
desired; see photo.

◆ ❖ ◆

*These wrapped ornaments
also look great plain, without
the roses and leaves.*

◆ ❖ ◆

Painted Cabin Tinware

MATERIALS (for two)

Two purchased 9" blue
   tin plates
Acrylic paints: black, blue,
   brown, burgundy, green,
   orange, white
Manila folder
Heavy-duty craft knife
Toothbrush
Matte spray

DIRECTIONS

1. Paint both sides of one plate burgundy and both sides of other plate green. Allow to dry.

2. To make stencils, transfer tree, snowman and hat patterns onto manila folder. Using a craft knife, cut out.

3. Place tree stencils on burgundy plate. Place snowman and hat stencils on green plate. Paint as desired; see photo. Allow to dry.

4. Place plates right side up. Dilute white paint. Dip toothbrush in paint and run finger over bristles to splatter paint as desired. Allow to dry. Finish with matte spray.

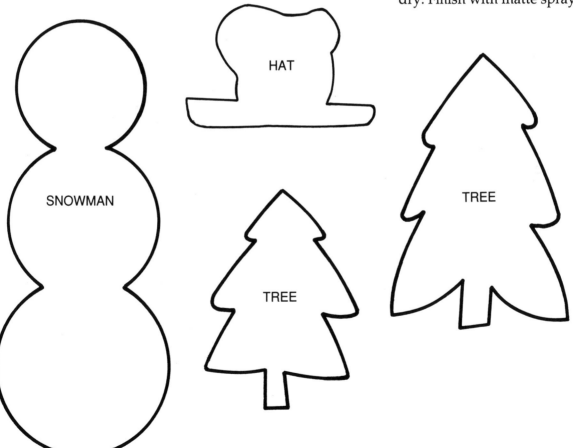

HAT

SNOWMAN

TREE

TREE

page 125

Beaded Victorian Star

MATERIALS

10" square of 36-gauge
  tooling brass
28" of 18-gauge brass wire
Burgundy acrylic paint
Brass paint
30–40 each green and red
  seed beads
Matte spray
Super glue
Needle-nose pliers
Soldering iron and solder

DIRECTIONS

1. Transfer star pattern three times onto brass. With wrong side up, place brass on a stack of paper. Emboss each star according to pattern. Cut out.

2. Cut brass wire in half. Using needle-nose pliers, twist wire lengths together. To make a spiral, loosely coil wire around thumb four times, leaving a 1" tail at one end. Set aside.

3. With embossed sides up, place first star over second star so that the points of the second star are between the points of the first star. Solder the two stars together. Place the soldered stars over the third star so that the points of the third star are aligned with the first star. Solder the third star to the second star. Slightly bend the points of the first star and the third star out.

4. Solder the 1" wire tail of the spiral between two aligned points of the first and third stars. Cover soldered spot with brass paint.

5. Lightly wash entire star tree topper with burgundy paint, wiping off excess. Allow to dry. Finish with matte spray.

6. Glue green and red seed beads onto first and second stars as desired. Finish with matte spray.

page 127

STAR

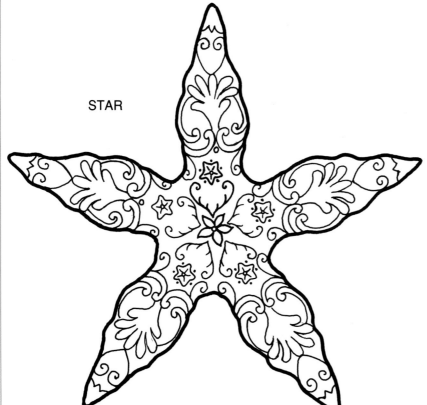

Wish Upon a Star

MATERIALS

Two 12" x 36" sheets of
   36-gauge tooling copper
5" square of 36-gauge
   tooling brass
18" of 14-gauge copper wire
Beading wire
One paper doily
Red acrylic paint
Gold leafing
One package of gold
   seed beads
Matte spray
Super glue
Soldering iron and solder

DIRECTIONS

1. Transfer star section
pattern on page 130, five
times, onto copper. Cut out.
Emboss scoring lines on each
section. With tabs on the left
side, fold each star section in
half on scoring line.

2. Place star sections, pointed
ends up, in a circle. Solder
the tab of one star section to
the back side of another star
section, forming a large star
with an opening in the
center.

3. String seed beads onto
beading wire to run the
length of the grooves in the
star. Cut strands to fit and
glue ends of thread to the
back of the star.

4. Bend wire into a spiral
with five-and-a-half loops.
Begin at bottom with half a
loop. Shape the next three
loops into spiral with a 3"
diameter. Fourth loop is 2½"
and top loop is 2" in
diameter. Leave a 2" wire tail
extending from the top of
spiral. Solder this tail to the
back of the molded star.

5. To make back piece for
star, trace around outside of
molded star onto copper. Cut
out this star shape and glue
to the back of the molded
star.

6. Transfer small star pattern
onto brass and doily. Cut out
one each. Align and glue
doily star to brass star.

7. Paint doily/brass star with
red paint. Allow to dry.
Cover red paint with gold
leafing, allowing the red
paint to show through.
Finish with matte spray.

SMALL STAR

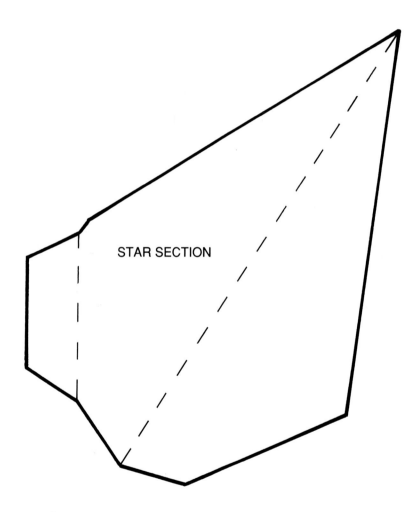

STAR SECTION

Delicate Doves

DOVE A

WING A

page
131

WING B

DOVE B

MATERIALS (for four)

12" square of 36-gauge
    tooling aluminum
Super glue
Hammer
¹⁄₁₆" awl
¹⁄₈" awl

DIRECTIONS

1. Transfer four dove patterns onto aluminum. Find more patterns on page 131.

2. With wrong side up, place aluminum on a stack of paper. Emboss according to patterns.

3. With right side up, place aluminum on a stack of paper. Punch holes according to patterns. Cut out.

4. Fold double wings in half and glue onto the back of each corresponding dove. Glue single wings onto the back of each corresponding dove.

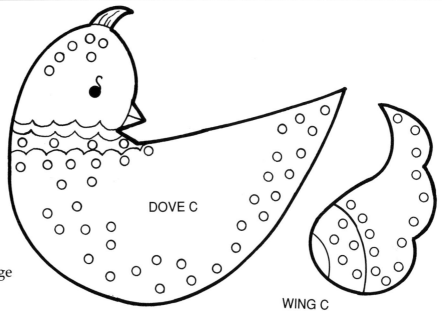

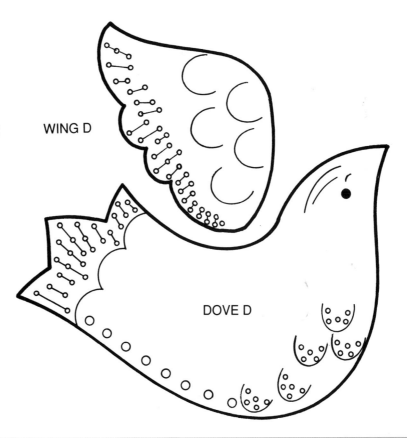

page 133

Christmas Bright

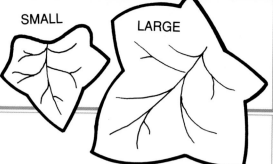

SMALL LARGE

MATERIALS

Two purchased metal
  candlestick holders
Three ¾" purchased
  wooden eggs
5" square of ¼" balsa wood
40" square of 24-gauge
  tooling copper
10 feet of 24-gauge copper
  wire
5 feet of 18-gauge copper
  wire
5 feet of 14-gauge copper
  wire
Acrylic paints: black, brown,
  cream, gray, green, red,
  white, yellow
Sixteen ⅛" red glass beads
Matte spray
Super glue
Needle-nose pliers
Heavy-duty craft knife
1/16" awl
Soldering iron and solder
Tin snips

DIRECTIONS

1. Cut two 12" lengths and six
6" lengths of 14-gauge copper
wire. Using needle-nose
pliers, twist the two 12"
lengths together. Using two
at a time, twist the 6" lengths
together. Bend the twisted
lengths according to stand
diagram.

To assemble stand, solder the
three 6" lengths to the bottom
center of the 12" length.
Solder the two candlestick
holders to the top of the 12"
length. Refer to diagram for
placement.

2. Transfer nine large and
fifteen small leaf patterns
onto copper. Cut out.

3. Cut twelve 1" and thirteen
2" lengths of 24-gauge wire;
set remaining wire aside.
Solder one length of wire to
the center back of each leaf,
reserving one 2" length.

4. Using needle-nose pliers,
wrap wire tails around stand
as desired; see photo. Solder
each wire tail in place to the
wire stand. For perch, bend
the remaining 2" length into
an "L" shape. Solder to center
top of stand.

5. Shape 18-gauge wire into a
nest. Weave the remaining
24-gauge wire around the
18-gauge wire. Solder nest to
middle of stand.

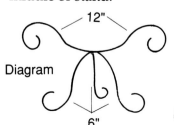

12"

Diagram

6"

6. Using craft knife, cut out
bird and wing patterns from
balsa wood. Glue wings to
bird according to pattern.
Using awl, make a ¼" deep
hole in the center bottom of
bird.

7. Paint stand and
candlestick holders red.
Wash with diluted green
paint and wipe excess. Paint
the leaves green,
highlighting with white.
Paint bird as desired. Allow
to dry. Attach bird to wire
behind nest by inserting wire
into hole at bottom of bird.
Finish entire piece with
matte spray.

8. Paint wooden eggs cream.
Speckle with brown paint.
Allow to dry. Glue in nest.
Glue red beads onto leaves
as desired; see photo.

*page
135*

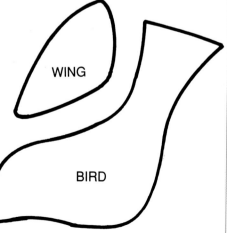

WING

BIRD

Dream Catcher

MATERIALS

14 feet of 18-gauge copper
    wire
7 feet of 24-gauge copper
    wire
11 feet of 32-gauge beading
    wire
Four 1" oblong beads
Four ¼" round beads
One ½" oblong bead
Needle-nose pliers
Tin snips

DIRECTIONS

1. Cut one 30" length of 18-gauge wire, set remaining aside. Using needle-nose pliers, bend wire into circle. Twist the ends of the wire and crimp to close.

2. Cut one 5-foot length of 24-gauge wire; set remaining aside. Loosely wrap 24-gauge wire around 18-gauge wire circle. Cut one 7-foot length of beading wire; set remaining aside. Loosely wrap beading wire around 18-gauge wire circle.

3. Cut four 16" lengths, four 10" lengths and four 8" lengths from remaining 18-gauge wire. Bend each 8" length into a one-loop shape, each 10" length into a heart and each 16" length into a three-loop shape. See Diagrams A and B. See Diagram C on page 138. To make joints on shapes, wrap a short length of remaining 24-gauge wire several times around intersecting 18-gauge wires. Refer to diagrams for joint placement.

page 137

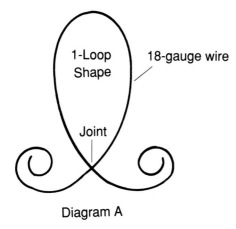

Diagram A

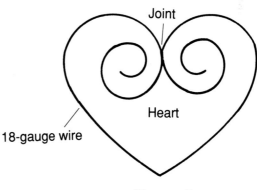

Diagram B

4. Referring to Diagram D, attach the hearts and the three-loop shapes with 24-gauge wire to the 18-gauge wire circle. Adjust shapes to fit, if necessary. Attach one-loop shapes to center of wreath, joining together as indicated. Adjust one-loop shapes to fit if necessary.

5. String one oblong bead onto a 5" length of beading wire. Place bead in middle of wire and thread one end of the wire through the bead again to hold it in place. Center the bead in the middle of a three-loop shape. Wrap wire tails around either end of loop to secure. Repeat with remaining 1" oblong beads. Repeat with round beads and ½" oblong beads, referring to diagram for placement.

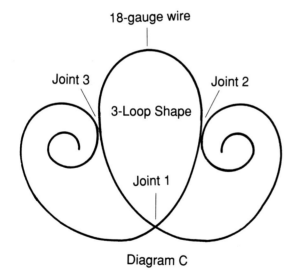

Diagram C

Diagram D

General Instructions

Adhesives and Glues

Spray adhesive is used to adhere two sheets of metal foil together in some projects. Following the manufacturer's instructions, spray one piece of foil with adhesive. Center second piece of foil over top of first and press in place. Make sure alignment is accurate as the foil bonds upon contact. Using scissors, trim the edges of the foils to match, if necessary. Super glue is also used in many projects and will provide a good strong hold. In no case should an adhesive or glue be substituted for soldering.

Antiquing

Use all chemicals outdoors or in a well-ventilated area, preferably with a fan. Face masks are also recommended.

Copper patina is used to make copper appear as if it has been weathered for years. Liver of sulphur (sulphurated potash) is an oxidizing agent that will turn the copper black. Both are chemicals that react with the metal to bring out the natural colors in it. In the case of copper patina, some projects will call for more than one coat to create a darker green color. Some projects may also require that the copper is first soaked in vinegar before applying the patina. This is done to remove the finish on the copper and to create blue hues along with the green. A small amount of liver of sulphur will provide desired results. Liver of sulphur gives off hydrogen sulfide gas, which not only smells unpleasant, but also is poisonous. When using these, carefully follow manufacturer's instructions.

Characteristics of Aluminum, Brass and Copper

Aluminum will not tarnish and does not require polishing or finishing.

Brass does not tarnish as quickly as copper.

Copper can be patinated, antiqued and heat-colored. To slow the tarnishing of brass and copper, polish with steel wool, then apply several coats of matte spray.

Cutting Metal

Use an old or inexpensive pair of scissors to cut lightweight metals. Tin snips should be used to cut heavyweight metals. To avoid short, jagged edges, keep the scissors or tin snips deep in the cut and do not withdraw the blades until the entire cut is completed.

Embossing

Embossing is indicated on the patterns by a thin, solid line. Emboss the pattern before cutting it out. Trace the embossing pattern onto a piece of tracing paper. Tape the paper in the appropriate place on the metal to be embossed. Place the metal on a stack of paper. Embossing can be done with a tin tool, a ball-point pen or a pencil. Simply trace the paper pattern onto the tin. Tracing the pattern on the metal right side up will give indented embossing. Tracing the pattern on the metal wrong side up will create raised embossing. Tracing the pattern several times will create a deeper line and will make the detail stand out more. Wipe the metal with a soft cloth to remove pen or pencil marks. A dry ballpoint pen also works well since it will not leave any ink behind.

Heat-Coloring

Heat-coloring must be done before soldering or the solder will melt.

This method uses carefully controlled heat to bring out color in copper. Use a gas range or Bunsen burner. Always hold the copper over the heat with a pair of metal tongs with plastic handles. A little heat will bring out a deep bronze color. Additional heat will bring out shades of purple and aqua. Keep the heat moving and do not overheat an area. Overheating will scorch the metal and all the color will be lost. Practice heat coloring on scraps of copper first.

Indentations

Indentations are indicated on patterns by small solid dots. Indent the pattern before cutting it out. Indentations are made with either a 1⁄16" or a 1⁄8" awl. Place the metal to be indented on a stack of paper. Following the indentation pattern, place the awl over the dot and press firmly.

Matte Spray

Clear matte finish spray is used to finish almost every project. The matte spray seals paints, patinas and other antquing methods. Matte spray will also delay the tarnishing process that occurs naturally on brass and copper. When applying seed beads, matte spray is used before *and* after gluing the beads in place to increase adherence.

Painting and Finishing

Many different types of paints are used in these projects for various effects. Copper paint and brass paint match the color of copper and brass almost perfectly. They are often used to cover soldering points. Acrylic paints are also used and can be applied with either brushes or sponges. Before applying acrylic paints, clean the surface of the metal with fine steel wool. In many projects a primer is used before applying paints.

Splatter painting is a technique that uses a toothbrush. Dip the toothbrush bristles into the paint and then run your finger over the bristles to splatter-paint your project. When the paints have dried, they are sealed with either a matte spray or a lacquer finish as specified in each project. In all cases, follow the manufacturer's instructions for paints and finishes.

Primer Spray

Apply metal primer before painting. It is used to improve the application and adhesion of acrylic paints.

Punching Holes

Punched holes are indicated on patterns with small open circles. Punch before cutting out the project. Copy the circle pattern onto tracing paper. Tape the paper over the tin to be punched. Place the metal to be punched on a stack of paper. A magazine or several sections of newspaper will work well. Following the punch pattern, first make a small indentation on the metal with an awl. Then place the awl over the indentation and gently tap with a hammer to make a hole. Use consistent pressure to assure uniform holes.

Scoring Lines

A broken line (– – – –) indicates scoring lines. These lines are used on crafts that require bending the metal to shape the project. Score the lines deeply with an embossing tool. Place a ruler along the line and bend the tin over it. This will give you corners with straight, sharp edges.

Solder

Resin core solder is used in all projects requiring solder.

Soldering

All soldering must be done before antiquing, painting or finishing. We recommend using a face mask while soldering to avoid breathing in lead fumes.

Use a soldering iron instead of a soldering gun. A soldering iron is easier to control. Touch the iron to the spot on the metal to be soldered, then touch the solder to the hot spot on the metal. If you have never used a soldering iron before, practice on scraps. You will quickly master the use of the iron. A little solder goes a long way. If you do make a mistake, touch the iron to the solder. The heat will melt the solder again and enable you to remove it. The soldering spot can be covered up with a variety of metallic paints that will blend with the metal almost perfectly. Soldering may cause the metal to tarnish. If this occurs, use fine steel wool to gently clean the tarnished spot.

Steel Wool

Very fine steel wool, 0000 grade, is used for cleaning and polishing. It is a good idea to clean all projects with steel wool before antiquing or painting. This will remove any dirt or oil from your hands that could be present on the surface of the metal. For projects that are not antiqued or painted, gently polish the surface to restore the metal's original luster. Also use steel wool to clean a metal surface that has been tarnished from soldering.

Tools

You will need the following basic tools for the projects in this book: tin snips, an old pair of scissors, super glue, a soldering iron and solder, a small awl, a hammer, a hardwood hammering board and needle-nose pliers. Keeping these tools in a convenient location will facilitate your work and make it more enjoyable.

Tracing Patterns

Trace patterns onto tracing paper. Tape pattern over metal. Using a ballpoint pen or a pencil, trace the pattern onto the metal. For a deeper indentation, trace over the pattern several times.

METRIC EQUIVALENCY CHART

MM-Millimetres   CM-Centimetres

INCHES TO MILLIMETRES AND CENTIMETRES

INCHES	MM	CM	INCHES	CM	INCHES	CM
⅛	3	0.3	9	22.9	30	76.2
¼	6	0.6	10	25.4	31	78.7
⅜	10	1.0	11	27.9	32	81.3
½	13	1.3	12	30.5	33	83.8
⅝	16	1.6	13	33.0	34	86.4
¾	19	1.9	14	35.6	35	88.9
⅞	22	2.2	15	38.1	36	91.4
1	25	2.5	16	40.6	37	94.0
1¼	32	3.2	17	43.2	38	96.5
1½	38	3.8	18	45.7	39	99.1
1¾	44	4.4	19	48.3	40	101.6
2	51	5.1	20	50.8	41	104.1
2½	64	6.4	21	53.3	42	106.7
3	76	7.6	22	55.9	43	109.2
3½	89	8.9	23	58.4	44	111.8
4	102	10.2	24	61.0	45	114.3
4½	114	11.4	25	63.5	46	116.8
5	127	12.7	26	66.0	47	119.4
6	152	15.2	27	68.6	48	121.9
7	178	17.8	28	71.1	49	124.5
8	203	20.3	29	73.7	50	127.0

YARDS TO METRES

YARDS	METRES	YARDS	METRES	YARDS	METRES	YARDS	METRES	YARDS	METRES
⅛	0.11	2⅛	1.94	4⅛	3.77	6⅛	5.60	8⅛	7.43
¼	0.23	2¼	2.06	4¼	3.89	6¼	5.72	8¼	7.54
⅜	0.34	2⅜	2.17	4⅜	4.00	6⅜	5.83	8⅜	7.66
½	0.46	2½	2.29	4½	4.11	6½	5.94	8½	7.77
⅝	0.57	2⅝	2.40	4⅝	4.23	6⅝	6.06	8⅝	7.89
¾	0.69	2¾	2.51	4¾	4.34	6¾	6.17	8¾	8.00
⅞	0.80	2⅞	2.63	4⅞	4.46	6⅞	6.29	8⅞	8.12
1	0.91	3	2.74	5	4.57	7	6.40	9	8.23
1⅛	1.03	3⅛	2.86	5⅛	4.69	7⅛	6.52	9⅛	8.34
1¼	1.14	3¼	2.97	5¼	4.80	7¼	6.63	9¼	8.46
1⅜	1.26	3⅜	3.09	5⅜	4.91	7⅜	6.74	9⅜	8.57
1½	1.37	3½	3.20	5½	5.03	7½	6.86	9½	8.69
1⅝	1.49	3⅝	3.31	5⅝	5.14	7⅝	6.97	9⅝	8.80
1¾	1.60	3¾	3.43	5¾	5.26	7¾	7.09	9¾	8.92
1⅞	1.71	3⅞	3.54	5⅞	5.37	7⅞	7.20	9⅞	9.03
2	1.83	4	3.66	6	5.49	8	7.32	10	9.14

Index